THE COMPLETE
AVOCADO
COOKBOOK

MURDOCH BOOKS®

Sydney • London • Vancouver • New York

THE COMPLETE
AVOCADO
COOKBOOK

CHRISTINE HEASLIP

MURDOCH BOOKS®
Sydney • London • Vancouver • New York

CONTENTS

INTRODUCTION

The avocado is a gourmet food which is natural, wholesome, easy to prepare and not too expensive to buy. Above all else, the avocado is remarkably versatile. The variety of recipes in this book reflects the great adaptability of the avocado, which I feel most cooks have not yet even begun to realise. If you have an avocado on hand, you have the basis for any number of quick, wholesome family meals; you also have a splendid ingredient for whipping up a 'dressy sauce' or providing extravagant touches to a special meal. All the recipes are original creations resulting from my own experimentation with avocados. There is a recipe for all tastes, all occasions and for all cooks, be you a chef of the highest standard, a person who simply enjoys cooking or someone who merely cooks to eat. You and your guests will be surprised and delighted at some of the spectacular and unusual ways of cooking and presenting this beautiful fruit.

Banavo Crepe

Most people use avocados in fairly simple ways; tossed in a salad, pureed for dips, sliced on toast or enhanced with a little lemon juice or dressing. Most would agree these are the best ways of eating avocados. I like to use avocado as a substitute for butter or margarine on bread, dry biscuits or toast. One of my favourite milkshakes is made with avocado and sweetened with a little honey, again a simple use for the humble avocado, and from one avocado you have enough to make four milkshakes which is good value! However, a little-known but most rewarding way of using avocados is in desserts. Their smooth, creamy texture lends a particular richness to many sweet dishes. They can simply be diced and included in a fruit salad, blended in a sauce to pour over fruit (bananas are especially delicious topped with this) or pureed with other ingredients to produce a rich flan or cheesecake filling. Unaccountably the avocado is not widely used in sweet dishes. Perhaps the most stunning desserts in this book, both for their taste and appearance, are Green Gateau and Almondine Avocado Meringue. They are great fun to cook and present, as I am sure you will discover. Try substituting avocado in some of your favourite dessert recipes!

Of all the main meals my favourite is undoubtedly the Crusty Stuffed Avocado. It was a great thrill to discover this tempting way of presenting avocados as a whole. In all recipes I have been aware to provide a broad spectrum, to allow people with all sorts of food preferences the opportunity to cook with avocados. You will find meals including red meat, chicken, seafood, vegetables, different cheeses, nuts and fruits. Recipes can be fun to alter and change to suit your individual taste and don't feel inhibited to do so with my recipes in this book.

In all recipes I have used as much as possible fresh, wholesome ingredients. Wholemeal flour is used rather than white flour, honey or raw sugar rather than refined (fruit sugar is readily available these days and is a good alternative to sugar too), fresh fruit, vegetables and herbs, very little salt and, in general, no highly refined or processed products. The recipes do lend themselves to be altered to suit your own taste. Please consider the following points when altering recipes: if you substitute white flour for wholemeal, use a little extra as wholemeal flour more readily absorbs liquid; if using honey instead of sugar, you will need slightly more dry ingredients to achieve the same consistency. If you add salt, add it at the end of the cooking time, as salt will destroy a lot of the vitamins and minerals and also toughens the foods you are cooking. Always taste your meal before adding salt, as often you will find you don't need any. A squirt of lemon juice is a good substitute for salt with particular foods, and especially so for avocados.

Though justifiably considered a delicacy, avocados are also nutritious and easily digestible which makes them an ideal food for babies and young children. Mashed or pureed, alone or in combination with other ingredients, they can be served to babies as one of their very first foods. Fruits are a good food to start with for baby's first foods, providing nutrition with easy digestibility. Avocado and banana are a nice combination, avocado mashed with a little fresh orange juice, avocado and mango, just to mention a few. Once a baby starts on other foods, the avocado can be mashed with natural yoghurt and pureed with soft salad vegetables, such as sprouts, grated carrot or cucumber.

Cooking with avocados needs a special mention and a few words of caution. The flavour of the avocado is definitely altered with the application of heat and certain nutrients are lost, as they are in all cooked food. But this does provide another avenue for the use of avocados and can be done successfully. The flavour can become bitter if avocado dishes are overcooked and a cooked avocado recipe should never be reheated, as the flavour will certainly be spoilt.

Avocado added to hot soups in their last stages, either in a pureed form or pieces, is an ideal meal and a meal with the minimum amount of heat applied. The recipe for Fried Avocado is another cooked meal which retains flavour and nutrition as it is sauteed very quickly. In fact, all of the cooked meals within these pages have been chosen bearing in mind that avocados should have as little cooking time as is possible.

The chapter headings are a guide only; you will find that most of the recipes can be readily adapted to different types of meals. Most of the entrees, for instance, if made in larger quantities, will stand very nicely as lunches or main meals. Some desserts, such as the fruit salad, make delightful summer breakfasts. So use your own style and imagination to get the most out of this book!

I hope you will find, as I have, that these recipes are as enjoyable to prepare as they are delicious to eat.

ABOUT THE AVOCADO

The avocado is native to Mexico and Central America. Indeed its name comes from the ancient Aztec name for the fruit, *ahuacatl*. By the time Columbus discovered America the avocado had spread to the north of the continent and south as far as Peru. It was later introduced to the West Indies in the early 16th century.

The trees are mostly evergreen and can grow to a height of around 12 metres. There are over 70 recognised varieties of avocado in Australia alone and the fruit is exceedingly variable in shape, size and colour. The three main commercial varieties are Fuerte, Sharwil and Hass.

Fuerte (hybrid)

This avocado has a classic pear shape, with a fairly smooth, dark green skin, which dulls as the fruit ripens. Best supply is from March until July.

Sharwil

This variety is more oval in shape and does not have a thin neck. The skin is rougher in comparison to the Fuerte. Availability is from May until July.

Hass

This is a smaller variety than the Sharwil or Fuerte and the skin is rough and more a purple/black colour when ripe. Best supply is from July until November.

Another common variety is the cocktail avocado ('kuke'), which is not a separate variety, but merely an immature avocado. It is a small bullet-shaped avocado. Because it has virtually no seed it is well suited to being sliced, served whole and presented in a multitude of ways.

The three main varieties: Hass (top left), Sharwil (top right) and Fuerte (bottom).

Photo courtesy The Committee of Direction of Fruit Marketing

NUTRITIONAL FACTS

Vitamins and minerals

The avocado supplies vitamins A (in the form of carotene), seven of the eight B complex, C and E plus vital minerals including potassium, phosphorus, magnesium, iron and several trace elements.

Protein and fibre

Rich in protein, it is important to note that it is a complete protein, containing all nine of the essential amino acids required for the manufacture of new tissue in the body. Avocados provide valuable dietary fibre, despite their smooth texture.

Kilojoules

The kilojoules in an avocado vary according to the size of the fruit, but an average half has 750 kilojoules (or 180 calories — about the same as 25 g of butter or margarine). Substitution of avocado for butter or margarine is ideal.

Fat and cholesterol

The fat contained in the avocado is a mono-unsaturated fat which actually decreases cholesterol levels in the bloodstream. This fat is also found in olives, olive oil, peanuts and peanut oil. The National Heart Foundation of Australia has granted approval to advertise this fact.

USEFUL HINTS

☐ Avocados will discolour easily once cut, but you can deal with this problem by:
coating with lemon juice using a pastry brush;
covering with very thin slices of lemon; and
leaving the seed in one half of the avocado which will slow down discoloration a little.
☐ Avocado pieces can be frozen fairly successfully if tossed with a good amount of lemon juice and put into freezer bags. Once thawed, the avocado can be used for purees, sauces, dips or any dish where appearance is not important.
☐ To speed the ripening process of an avocado, put it in a brown paper bag with a ripe banana and store the bag at room temperature. Check every day for ripeness.
☐ When cooking with avocado, it is important not to boil whatever it is in or to overcook it, as the unique and subtle flavour of the avocado is easily destroyed. They can develop a bitter flavour if cooked improperly.
☐ Uncooked dessert dishes will usually keep well in the refrigerator for two days. Cooked dishes will be edible cold the next day, but reheating will often destroy the flavour.

Selection and storage

☐ Mature but firm fruit will often take 4–5 days to ripen. Ripen them in a cool, airy spot at room temperature.
☐ Ripe and ready to eat fruit can be stored in the refrigerator for 4–5 days. Be wary of overripe fruit. To test for ripeness, cradle the avocado in the palm of your hand and gently press with the thumb at the stem end. If the flesh yields to your touch, the avocado is ready to eat.

Preparation

☐ Cut avocado lengthways into halves.
☐ Twist to separate.
☐ Insert a sharp knife into the seed, twist and lift seed out.
☐ To make avocado balls use a melon baller or round metal half teaspoon measure.
☐ To peel avocado, strip skin from fruit beginning at narrow end.
☐ Cavity side down, cut lengthways or, for crescents, crosswise; to dice or cube cut both ways.
☐ To make rings, cut around avocado crosswise with tip of knife to form rings, then remove skin.

Warning

Care has to be taken when buying avocados that are out of season or imported. If an avocado is picked too early — so that its oil content is at a level insufficient to allow for the full development of its flavour during ripening — or if it is picked too late in the season — when it is stale — its flavour will be affected. In some cases imported avocados that may have been placed in cold storage before being presented for sale have been known to overripen. This can result in an avocado that quickly browns when cut open, making for an unattractive appearance and an unsavoury taste.

Avocado cutting techniques

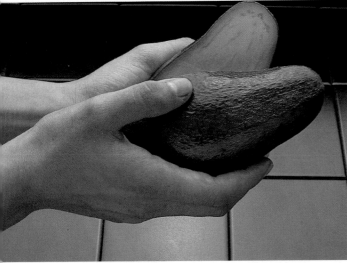

1 *Cut avocado lengthways Twist the halves apart
Cut into the seed and lift*

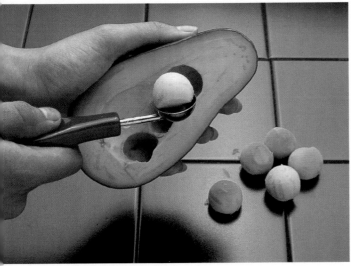

2 *Preparing avocado balls*

3 *Cutting crescents and half rings*

SOME SPECIAL INGREDIENTS

Agar-Agar

Sea vegetable gelatine. High in calcium and other minerals.

Balsamic Vinegar

A specialty vinegar made from the concentrated must of white grapes which is matured in casks for up to 25 years.

Capers

The unopened flower buds of the caper bush, commonly grown in the Mediterranean.

Coriander

A herb similar to parsley when fresh, but widely used in Indian cooking as a spice in powder form.

Cumin

An aromatic Indian spice.

Julienne Strips

Vegetables sliced into very thin 2 cm strips that require very little cooking.

Pepitas

Edible green pumpkin seeds.

Pine Nuts

Kernels from the cone of the Mediterranean umbrella pine tree.

Pita Bread

Flat bread which is used widely in Mediterranean and Middle Eastern countries.

Sorrel

A herb widely used with fish because of its distinct lemon flavour; similar in appearance to English spinach.

Tahini

A paste made from sesame seeds, much like peanut butter but very smooth.

Tamari

Similar to soy sauce but tamari is aged longer and has a slightly different flavour.

ENTREES

This section contains a wide variety of recipes, enabling you to use avocados as individually and imaginatively as you wish. The traditional avocado half is presented with some interesting variations. Some of these entrees make delightful lunches if served in larger quantities. For instance, the Gardinera Avocado Mini Pizza and the Crumble Topped Avocado Quiche both make a satisfying, complete meal with the addition of fresh vegetables or a light salad.

There is a basic avocado soup recipe as well as one for Sorrel and Avocado Soup. Variations to the basic soup recipe are not included, but almost anything can be added to suit individual tastes, such as zucchini, prawns, cheese or herbs.

AVOCADO SOUP

A superb soup served hot or cold.

2 avocados	¼ cup cream
2 cups chicken or strong vegetable stock	salt and freshly ground pepper
juice ½ lemon	

Puree avocado with stock and lemon juice in blender. Heat gently until hot. Don't boil.

Season and add cream before serving. If serving cold, there is no need to cook the soup, just puree as above and add seasonings and cream.

Note: This soup can be served with croutons or a crusty breadstick and sprinkled with chopped watercress.

Serves 4

SORREL AND AVOCADO SOUP

The superb lemon flavour of fresh sorrel blends beautifully with avocado. English spinach can be substituted.

2 avocados	freshly ground pepper
150 mL cream	dash lemon juice, if
500 g fresh sorrel leaves	spinach is used
50 g butter	

Mash avocados and mix with a little of the cream.

Shred sorrel leaves and gently cook in butter for 5 minutes. Cool. Put stock in blender with cooked sorrel and puree until smooth.

Return to saucepan and heat again over moderate heat, adding cream and pepper at the very end with the mashed avocado. Serve hot.

Serves 4

AVOCADO CHOWDER

A good substantial soup for winter nights with avocado and potato as the main ingredients, bacon pieces to add that extra flavour and cheese to top it off.

6 large potatoes, peeled and cut into small cubes
3 bay leaves
6 rashers bacon, rind removed and finely chopped
40 g butter
2 large onions, finely chopped
½ cup finely chopped celery
2 cups milk
1 cup cream
pinch or two nutmeg
salt and freshly ground pepper
2 large avocados, mashed
200 g Gouda cheese, grated, to serve
sweet paprika to garnish

Cook potatoes with bay leaves in enough water to just cover them, until potatoes are soft. Drain.

In a large saucepan cook chopped bacon in its own fat. Add butter, onions and celery and cook until soft.

Heat milk, cream and nutmeg gently together and then add all remaining ingredients, including the mashed avocado. Bring to the boil, turn off the heat, put the lid on and stand for 20 minutes to allow the flavours to blend together. In fact, this soup is best served the next day. If you do serve it the next day, save the addition of the avocado until it has been reheated.

Top with grated Gouda cheese and sprinkle with a little paprika to serve.

Serves 6

FISH AND AVOCADO BISQUE

4 cups water	30 g butter
½ cup white wine	2 large avocados, chopped
2 onions, thinly sliced	200 g cooked prawns
1 teaspoon black peppercorns	¼ cup cream salt
300 g fish fillets	4 prawns and 4 slices
6 shallots, finely chopped	avocado for garnish
1 tablespoon dried tarragon	

Put 2 cups of the water, wine, sliced onions and peppercorns in a saucepan and slowly bring to the boil. Add fish fillets and simmer uncovered over a low heat for approximately 10 minutes. Remove fillets with a slotted spoon. Remove bones and break up fillets slightly. Strain and reserve stock.

Saute shallots and tarragon in butter for 2 minutes. Add reserved stock, remaining water and fish. Bring to boil and simmer covered for 10 minutes. Blend soup with chopped avocados until smooth. Return to saucepan; add cooked prawns and reheat gently. Lastly add cream and salt to taste. Garnish each bowl of soup with a whole prawn and a semi-circle of avocado hung on side of bowl.

Serves 4

HOT AVOCADO AND CORN DIP

A warm dip is perfect for a cool evening.

40 g butter
6 cloves garlic, crushed
2 stalks celery, finely chopped
2 cobs corn, scraped
450 mL cream
2 avocados, mashed
3 anchovies, well mashed
freshly ground pepper
Parmesan cheese, grated

Melt butter and saute crushed garlic, celery and corn for 10 minutes. Add cream and heat well. When very hot, add mashed avocado and anchovies and stir until well combined. Grind in some fresh pepper just before serving. Some Parmesan cheese can be sprinkled on too.

Serve with various vegetable sticks, such as carrot, button mushrooms, broccoli flowers, fresh asparagus and, a must with this dip, chunks of French bread to dunk.

Note: If you like a thicker dip, stir in 2 tablespoons cornflour or arrowroot made into a paste with a little water.

Serves 4-6

AVOCADO ROLLED SUSHI

This delicious combination of rice, avocado and peanut sauce rolled in seaweed is Japanese in origin. You can buy the nori (dried seaweed) in specialist delicatessens.

PEANUT SAUCE	FILLING
½ onion finely chopped	½ teaspoon tamari
1 tablespoon oil	2 cups cooked brown rice
2 tablespoons peanut butter	6 sheets nori
pinch chilli powder	juice 1 lemon
½ cup coconut milk	1 large avocado, thickly sliced

Cook onion in oil for a few minutes. Stir in peanut butter and chilli powder and then gradually add the coconut milk, stirring constantly, to form a thick sauce. If too thick, add a little water, but the sauce should be thick enough to not run when spread on the nori.

To make the filling, mix tamari through cooked brown rice. Lay each nori sheet on a board and, with a pastry brush, lightly brush nori with lemon juice. Over three-quarters of nori sheet, spread a thin, even layer of peanut sauce. Lay brown rice evenly on top and, in centre of sheet, lay 2 slices of avocado in a line. Roll nori sheet up to form a cylinder.

Cover nori with plastic wrap and rest for at least 30 minutes before serving. To serve, cut each nori into 3 equal-sized mini-rolls with a very sharp knife and arrange decoratively on a Japanese dish.

VARIATION

In place of peanut sauce, a little horseradish cream can be spread on nori sheet.

Serves 6

Avocado Rolled Sushi

SCALLOP AND AVOCADO MOUSSELINE WITH LEMON AND DILL SAUCE

A combination of delicate flavours makes this mousseline a perfect beginning to any gourmet dinner.

300 g fresh scallops,
   cleaned and cooked
1 egg
1 egg white (reserve yolk
   for sauce)
1 cup cream

2 medium avocados
pinch nutmeg
salt and freshly ground
   pepper
few sprigs watercress for
   garnish

Blend all ingredients, reserving 6 thin slices of avocado, in a blender or food processor until smooth. Squeeze a little lemon juice over reserved avocado. Pour mixture into 6–8 individual lightly greased souffle dishes or other moulds, cover with lightly buttered foil and bake in a dish half filled with water. Bake at 180°C (350°F) for 50 minutes.

LEMON AND DILL SAUCE

20 g softened butter
1 tablespoon plain flour
1 egg yolk
1¼ cups cream
3 tablespoons lemon juice

finely grated rind ½ lemon
2 tablespoons fresh dill or
   1 teaspoon dried dill
salt and pepper

Mix softened butter, flour and egg yolk with fork.

Heat cream, lemon juice and rind in heavy-based saucepan. When simmering, beat in butter mixture with whisk or beater until it forms a thick sauce of pouring consistency.

Stir in dill and season to taste.

To serve mousseline, pour lemon and dill sauce into centre of each entree plate, invert mousseline onto sauce and garnish with a sprig of watercress and reserved avocado.

Serves 6–8

Scallop and Avocado Mousseline with Lemon and Dill Sauce

1 *Place moulds in pan of water to cook*

2 *Whisk butter mixture into sauce*

GUACAMOLE WITH TOFU AND CARAWAY

For those who eat tofu regularly, this tasty recipe will become part of your repertoire. Children find this recipe very palatable and it can be spread onto toast or crispbreads or used as a dip.

1 large avocado
250 g tofu
2 cloves garlic, crushed
4 tablespoons lemon juice
pinch cayenne pepper (optional)
1 teaspoon caraway seeds
salt and freshly ground pepper
1 medium-sized tomato, chopped very small

Mash avocado well with tofu and mix in crushed garlic, lemon juice, cayenne, caraway seeds, salt and pepper. Add chopped tomato. Allow to stand for at least 30 minutes to allow caraway seeds to permeate guacamole.

Makes 1½ cups

AVOCADO TOMATO FONDUE

40 g butter
2 tablespoons flour
1½ cups milk
2 cups grated cheddar cheese
100 g tomato paste
dash cayenne pepper
½ cup fresh basil, finely chopped
2 medium-sized avocados, pureed to a smooth
   consistency
½ lemon

Melt butter in a fondue pot or a heavy-based saucepan. Stir in flour, cook a minute. Add milk gradually, while stirring until thick and smooth. Remove from heat and stir in grated cheese, tomato paste, cayenne pepper and fresh basil. Add pureed avocados. Return to low heat and cook while stirring until hot. Squeeze in a dash or two of lemon juice before serving.

Serve with bread sticks, chunks of warm French bread, bread rolls or corn chips. Small button mushrooms, lightly cooked cauliflower or broccoli and fresh asparagus spears add crunchy variety.

Note: If you do not have a fondue pot, serve fondue in small quantities in warmed pottery bowls in order to keep fondue hot.

Makes 2½ cups

AVOCADO PATE

2 large avocados
4 hard-boiled eggs, finely chopped
2 tablespoons lemon juice
2 cloves garlic, crushed
2 teaspoons chopped parsley
1 tablespoon chopped fresh mint
salt and freshly ground pepper
¼ cup sour cream or mayonnaise
pinch sweet paprika

Cut avocados in half, remove seed and carefully scoop out flesh and put in a bowl. Save the avocado skins for serving.

Mash avocado with all remaining ingredients. Replace mixture into shells, smoothing down so as to keep avocado shape.

Garnish with lemon twist and a sprig of parsley and serve with Melba toast or crackers.

Note: Slight discoloration can occur if avocados are not freshly ripened.   Serves 4

PRAWN AND AVOCADO PATE

60 g butter
3 tablespoons plain flour
1 cup milk
½ cup sour cream
2 avocados
250 g small prawns, shelled
½ teaspoon Dijon mustard
freshly ground pepper
2 teaspoons gelatine
¼ cup water
¼ cup mayonnaise
1 tablespoon lemon juice
chopped parsley and ½ avocado to garnish

Melt butter and add flour. Remove from heat and gradually stir in milk and sour cream. Stir until well combined and sauce thickens. Simmer for 5 minutes over low heat. Cool slightly.

Blend sauce and avocado in a blender until smooth. Chop prawns finely, reserving 12 for garnish. Mix through avocado sauce. Add mustard and freshly ground pepper.

Sprinkle gelatine over water and dissolve over hot water. Add gelatine to avocado mixture. Cool to lukewarm. Mix through mayonnaise and lemon juice.

Spoon into 6 individual dishes or pate bowls and refrigerate for a few hours. Garnish with chopped parsley, 2 prawns each person and a little finely sliced avocado. Serve with Melba toast or crudites.

Note: a slight discoloration can occur if avocados are not freshly ripened.

Serves 6   *Prawn and Avocado Pate*

1 *Blend sauce and avocado till smooth*

2 *Mix chopped prawns through the avocado sauce*

AVOCADO WITH SALMON AND PEPPERCORNS

A perfect quick entree. The topping can be prepared well in advance and then simply warmed to serve.

2 tablespoons shallots, chopped
½ cup cream
pinch of ground nutmeg
pinch of fresh cracked pepper
50 g minced smoked salmon
1 level teaspoon pink peppercorns
1 tablespoon freshly grated Parmesan cheese
lettuce leaves, to serve
1 large avocado, halved and seeded

Warm the shallots, cream, nutmeg, pepper, salmon and peppercorns in a small saucepan over medium heat, stirring with a wooden spoon until almost boiling. Remove from the heat and stir in the Parmesan cheese.

Line 2 dishes with lettuce leaves, place the avocado halves over the lettuce, then spoon over the warm sauce. Alternatively, fan the peeled avocado onto a serving plate and spoon sauce over it. Garnish with a little extra cracked black pepper.

Serves 2

FRIED AVOCADO

Frying is probably the simplest way of cooking avocado. A lemon or Hollandaise sauce will make it dressier.

avocados, sliced crosswise
beaten egg
breadcrumbs (can be combined with sesame seeds, caraway seeds or a pinch or two of your favourite herb)
butter for frying

Dip avocado slices into egg, then breadcrumbs and fry gently until golden brown on both sides. Handle carefully so as not to break up the avocado.

Garnish with fresh dill or tarragon and a slice of lemon.

Fried Avocado

CRUMBLE TOPPED AVOCADO QUICHE

In the past few years quiches have become very popular. They provide an excellent vehicle for featuring the delicate flavour of the avocado.

PASTRY

250 g plain flour
200 g soft butter

FILLING

2 avocados
125 g cream cheese
4 eggs
1 cup cream, or ½ milk and ½ cream
pinch nutmeg
salt and freshly ground pepper
4 finely chopped shallots

CRUMBLE

2 tablespoons sesame seeds
½ cup breadcrumbs
60 g melted butter

Cut butter into flour with a long-bladed knife, then rub in with fingertips until it resembles breadcrumbs. Form into a ball, wrap in plastic wrap and chill for at least 1 hour before using.

Grease a pie dish or quiche tray and press pastry into dish with fingertips evenly. (This pastry has so much butter it is too crumbly to roll out, but you can use your favourite shortcrust pastry instead.) Prick all over with a fork and bake for 10 minutes at 200°C (400°F).

Blend avocado, cream cheese, eggs, cream, nutmeg and seasonings in blender until smooth. Mix in shallots and pour into pie crust. Bake at 180°C (350°F) for 30 to 40 minutes or until set.

Make crumble by tossing melted butter with seeds and breadcrumbs. Spread evenly over top of quiche when quiche is just starting to set (about 15 to 20 minutes) before end of cooking time. Crumble should be browned before removing quiche.

Note: Quiche can be allowed to cool down for about 15 minutes before serving as it is just as nice at room temperature. It will keep well for the next day too.

Serves 8–10

AVOCADO CHICKEN WALDORF

This combination of avocado, chicken, apple, celery, walnuts and mayonnaise can be served as a first course or as a salad.

200 g chopped chicken, cooked
2 avocados, chopped
1 small red apple, finely chopped
1 stalk celery, chopped
1 tablespoon lemon juice
½ cup mayonnaise
½ cup walnuts

Combine all ingredients. Serve on a lettuce leaf and garnish with one or two whole walnuts and avocado slices.

Serves 4

VOL-AU-VENTS

Vol-au-vents are ideal to have at a dinner party or with drinks. Try them filled with avocado, mushrooms, spring onions and bacon in a creamy sauce, or simply invent your own combination.

2 rashers bacon, rind removed and chopped finely
6 shallots, finely sliced
200 g button mushrooms, chopped small
2 avocados, chopped small
salt and freshly ground pepper
1 cup Bechamel Sauce (see recipe) with 1 teaspoon
   dried tarragon added
24 cocktail vol-au-vent cases
fresh tarragon or parsley for garnish

Cook bacon until just crisp in a pan in its own fat. Drain bacon and reserve fat. Cook shallots and mushrooms in reserved fat.

Combine bacon, cooked mushrooms, shallots, chopped avocados, salt and some freshly ground pepper. Add to bechamel sauce and heat combined filling while vol-au-vent cases are warming in oven — heat at 180°C (350°F) for about 5 minutes.

Spoon filling into cases and garnish with a little fresh tarragon or parsley.

Makes 24

INDIVIDUAL AVOCADO, CHICKEN AND ASPARAGUS TARTS

250 g shortcrust pastry
  (makes 8 × 10 cm tarts)
150 g cooked chicken,
  sliced thinly
1 avocado, sliced
  lengthways
12 asparagus spears
  (tinned or freshly
  cooked)

juice 1 small lemon
2 eggs, lightly beaten
70 mL milk
70 mL sour cream
freshly ground black
  pepper
2 pinches nutmeg

Line 6 greased individual tart moulds with shortcrust pastry. Place thinly sliced chicken in bottom of each pastry shell. Top with avocado slices and asparagus spears. Sprinkle with a little lemon juice.

Beat eggs with milk, sour cream, black pepper and nutmeg.

Carefully spoon custard over the filling in each pastry shell and bake at 220°C (425°F) for 10 minutes, then reduce to 180°C (350°F) for a further 10 minutes or until custard is set and pastry cooked.

Serves 6

GARDINERA AVOCADO MINI PIZZA

Fresh garden vegetables, avocado and cheese baked on pita bread all add up to a dish that's a great success with children. These little pizzas also make a good lunch.

2 mini-sized pieces of pita bread
1 avocado, thinly sliced
1 tomato, thinly sliced
1 zucchini, thinly sliced
1 onion, finely chopped
1 tablespoon finely chopped capsicum
1 tablespoon chopped parsley
2 tablespoons tomato paste
1 cup grated cheese, or ½ cup fresh Parmesan and
  ½ cup Cheddar cheese
optional: a few chopped olives as garnish

Mix all ingredients except cheese in a bowl. Spread evenly over pita bread, making sure it is covered right up to the edge. Top with sliced avocado and then grated cheese.

Put in preheated oven at 220°C (425°F), until cheese has melted and is bubbling and brown, or put under grill (not too close) until done.

Serves 2

Individual Avocado, Chicken and Asparagus Tarts　　　　　*Gardinera Avocado Mini Pizza*

AVOCADO GNOCCHI

2 avocados
250 g ricotta cheese
150 g fresh Parmesan
  cheese, grated

1 egg
¼ teaspoon nutmeg
50 g butter
plain flour

Mash avocados with the ricotta cheese, half the Parmesan cheese and the egg and nutmeg. Mix well.

Form the mixture into balls the size of small eggs, using a spoon and the palm of your hand to mould them. Roll balls lightly in the flour.

Bring a large pot of salted water to the boil and drop the gnocchi in, 4 or 5 at a time. Simmer gently until the gnocchi rise to the surface (about 2 minutes).

Remove from the pot with a slotted spoon and arrange in a well greased, flat oven dish. Melt butter and pour over the gnocchi; sprinkle with remaining Parmesan cheese.

Place under hot grill for a few minutes until cheese turns golden brown.

Variation: Serve with piquant Tomato-Herb Sauce.

TOMATO-HERB SAUCE

500 g tomatoes, chopped
1 bay leaf
1 small onion, chopped
1 tablespoon chopped
  parsley
¼ teaspoon dried basil
1 clove garlic, crushed
1 teaspoon sweet paprika
¼ cup red wine

Cook all ingredients together for about 1 hour or until sauce is thick. Stir occasionally.

Mixture can be pureed in a blender if a smooth sauce is preferred, but allow to cool a little first.

Note: For variation, ½ cup sour cream can be stirred in or ¼ cup ordinary cream. Two teaspoons of tomato paste can be added for a richer tomato flavour.

Serves 4–6

Avocado Gnocchi

Avocado al Pesto

AVOCADO CARBONARA

6 rashers bacon, rind
  removed and cut into
  thin strips
20 g butter
½ bunch shallots, finely
  chopped
½ green capsicum, thinly
  sliced
½ red capsicum, thinly
  sliced
2 avocados, chopped

½ cup cream
freshly ground black
  pepper
2 egg yolks
60 g Parmesan cheese,
  grated
250 g cooked pasta of your
  choice
1 level teaspoon sweet
  paprika

Cook bacon strips in their own fat over low heat until crisp. Remove bacon with slotted spoon. Set aside. Add butter to pan and saute chopped shallots and green and red capsicum for a couple of minutes. Mash or puree avocado with cream and black pepper. Toss bacon, cooked shallots and capsicum with avocado puree.

Mix egg yolks with half the grated Parmesan cheese and combine with avocado mixture. Toss pasta with sauce over a low heat until well combined and hot.

Serve immediately, garnish with remaining Parmesan cheese and sprinkle with sweet paprika.   Serves 6

AVOCADO AL PESTO

A classic Italian dressing served with a classic food.

1½ cups olive oil
8 cloves garlic, peeled
2 cups fresh basil leaves (increase for a thicker
  sauce)
⅔ cup freshly grated Parmesan cheese
2 large avocados, sliced
shredded lettuce or curly endive

Blend oil, garlic and basil in a blender until smooth and thick. Mix in grated cheese. Heat sauce in double boiler until hot, stirring constantly.

To serve, arrange sliced avocado on a bed of shredded lettuce or endive. Spoon hot sauce over avocado. A little cream may be added to sauce when heating.

Note: This sauce freezes well without the addition of the cream.

Serves 4

ASPARAGUS AVOCADO MUSHROOMS

The delicate flavours of avocado and asparagus are encased in open field-mushroom caps.

8 large mushrooms, stalks gently twisted out
4 fresh or tinned asparagus spears
1 avocado
juice 1 lemon
optional: dash or two of Tabasco sauce
freshly ground black pepper
grated cheese
sour cream and paprika to garnish

Arrange half the asparagus spears over mushrooms. Finely chop the remaining asparagus. Mash these with avocado, lemon juice, tabasco and a little freshly ground black pepper.

Pile into mushrooms, allowing mixture to sit slightly above level of the mushroom. Sprinkle over grated cheese and grill until bubbly.

Note: Can be served raw. Garnish with a little sour cream and paprika.

Serves 4

AVOCADO STUFFED POTATO

This makes a first course with a difference, and is a wonderful addition to most foods with which you would serve baked potatoes.

2 medium-sized sweet potatoes or ordinary potatoes
1 avocado
10 g butter
1 medium-sized onion, very finely chopped
salt and freshly ground pepper

Bake whole, unpeeled potatoes in 220°C (425°F) oven until soft, but firm enough to stuff. Cool.

Cut evenly in half and scoop out flesh, allowing a small rim inside potato for shape. Blend or mash avocado with potato flesh and mix with butter, onion and seasonings. Replace in potato shell and top with a little knob of butter, if desired. Bake at 200°C (400°F) until heated through and lightly browned on top. Dust with paprika.

Note: Grated cheese or breadcrumbs can be cooked on top when reheating. A dollop of sour cream completes the dish.

Serves 4

Asparagus Avocado Mushrooms

Avocado Stuffed Potato

MUSHROOM STUFFED AVOCADO

This dish is a delight for those who love the combination of garlic and mushrooms.

350 g mushrooms, sliced
2 cloves garlic, crushed
50 g butter
1 large avocado, halved

Saute mushrooms and garlic in butter until mushrooms are just tender but not mushy. Spoon into centre of avocado halves and top with cocktail sauce.

COCKTAIL SAUCE

½ cup cream
1 teaspoon tomato paste
2 teaspoons lemon juice
1 teaspoon tamari or soy sauce

½ teaspoon tarragon
4 drops Tabasco sauce
½ teaspoon sweet paprika
freshly ground pepper

Heat ingredients in saucepan until fairly hot. Do not boil. Cool slightly before serving. If a thicker sauce is desired, it can be thickened with a little arrowroot or cornflour. Garnish with slices of fresh mushroom and lemon.

Serves 2

Mushroom Stuffed Avocado

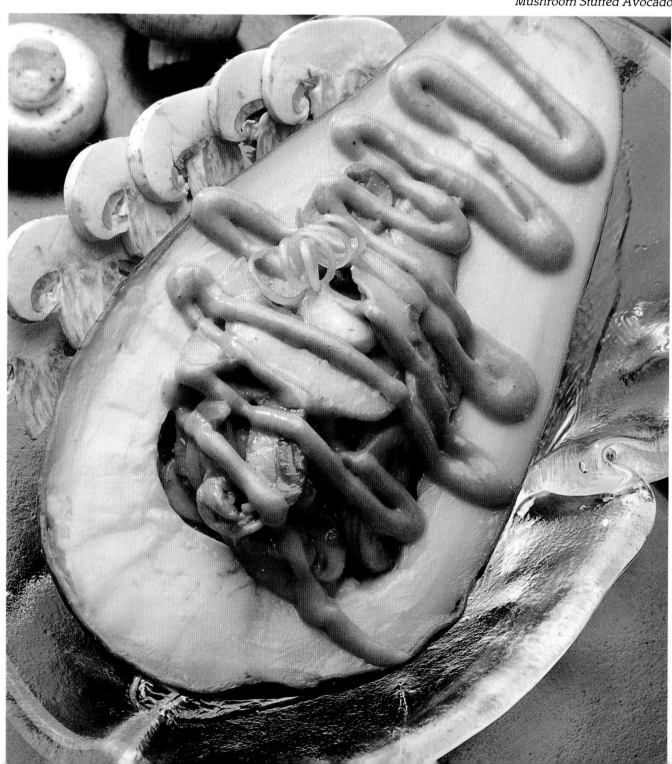

Avodamia Nest

AVODAMIA NEST

NEST

2 avocados
2 beaten eggs
ground raw macadamia nuts to coat
oil for frying

FILLINGS

1 medium onion, finely sliced
8 large mushrooms, finely sliced
20 g butter
sour cream to garnish
OR
1½ cups grated cheese
4 slices ham, finely chopped
2 stalks celery, finely chopped
OR
2 tomatoes, diced, or cherry tomatoes
4 shallots, finely chopped
½ teaspoon dried basil
1 clove garlic, crushed
125 g cream cheese, finely diced

Cut avocados in half, remove seeds and carefully peel away skin.

Dip avocado into beaten egg, then into ground macadamia nuts. Rather than move the avocado half around too much, it is easier to toss the nuts over it with a spoon.

Fry in shallow oil on both sides until golden brown.

Saute onions and mushrooms in a little butter until soft but not mushy.

Place in 'avodamia' nest and garnish with a swirl of sour cream and a sprinkling of paprika.

To make alternative fillings:

Toss cheese, ham and celery together and pile into avodamia nest. Grill under moderate heat until cheese is bubbling and browning slightly; or mix all ingredients together and pile into avodamia nest. Bake in a very hot oven until filling is heated through.

Note: If the last filling is used, don't brown the avodamia nest quite as much to allow for browning in the oven.

Serves 4

You can use your own imagination for fillings and toppings for this basic idea.

SALMON AND AVOCADO HOLLANDAISE

A combination of very thin slices of smoked salmon served on avocado and topped with Hollandaise sauce.

200 g smoked salmon, cut into thin strips
6 lettuce leaves
6 lemon twists and parsley to garnish
3 avocados, halved, seeded and thinly sliced

Twist thin strips of salmon and serve on lettuce leaves if desired. Spoon over sauce and garnish with a lemon slice, fresh parsley and avocado.

HOLLANDAISE SAUCE

180 g butter
3 egg yolks
salt and freshly ground pepper
1 tablespoon lemon juice

Melt the butter. Put eggs, seasonings and lemon juice in a blender and combine. Allow melted butter to cool for 1 minute.

While the blender is in motion, very gradually drip the melted butter through the hole in the lid until sauce is smooth. Serve immediately.

Note: This sauce can be temperamental if you're not used to dealing with emulsifying sauces. Just take it slowly, step by step.

Serves 6

LEMANGE AVOCADO

A refreshing change from the simple avocado vinaigrette.

3 avocado halves with seeds removed

DRESSING

4 tablespoons olive oil
4 tablespoons orange juice
3 tablespoons lemon juice
1 tablespoon honey
salt and freshly ground pepper

Shake all ingredients in a jar. Allow to stand for at least 30 minutes before using or, ideally, chill dressing before serving.

To serve, arrange avocado half on a lettuce or chicory leaf or in an avocado dish. Spoon over dressing and garnish with an orange slice and finely chopped parsley.

Serves 3

Salmon and Avocado Hollandaise

Crepes, pastries, roulades and many other interesting dishes are featured in this section. Some can be prepared in very little time; others need more of your attention. But always bear in mind the delicate flavour of the avocado and never reheat or overcook a meal, as it would be spoiled completely.

Crepes can be prepared ahead of time, and the avocado filling added just before serving. Remember that crepes are always more tasty when heated with the filling inside, rather than before the filling is added.

The Crusty Stuffed Avocado presents the avocado whole. It is a very substantial meal and lends itself to the inclusion of a filling to suit your own taste, be it seafood, poultry or vegetables.

FLAMED CHICKEN AND AVOCADO POULETTE

A simple dish of tender chicken fillets, avocados and shallots in a white wine and brandy sauce. Mushrooms or chicken livers can be added to make it more elaborate.

6 filleted chicken breasts
1½ cups white wine
6 tablespoons finely chopped shallots
2 teaspoons pickled peppercorns
60 g butter
2 large avocados, sliced
4 tablespoons brandy
2 cups cream
4 egg yolks
salt

Poach chicken fillets, 3 at a time, in white wine, adding a little more if evaporated by the time you cook next 3 fillets. This should take about 5 minutes on each side. When cooked, keep fillets warm in a casserole dish.

Add shallots and peppercorns to remaining wine liquid in pan and cook until liquid is reduced to about 1 cup.

Melt butter in a frying pan and gently toss avocado slices to warm through. Remove avocado with a slotted spoon and put with chicken. Warm brandy and add to remaining butter. Ignite and when flames subside, add cream and heat to just below boiling point. Remove from heat and allow to cool a little. Add beaten egg yolks, then shallots with peppercorns and reduced wine liquid.

Gently incorporate all ingredients well and pour over warmed chicken and avocado. Bake at 200°C (400°F) for approximately 15 minutes. Serve with buttered noodles or rice.

Note: 150 g chicken livers can be added by cooking them with the butter and adding the avocados at the end of the cooking time. Cook livers only until they change colour and then remove from heat and keep warm with chicken fillets.

Also 200 g button mushrooms can be added by cooking them with shallots, then adding them to warmed chicken fillets.

Serves 6

Flamed Chicken and Avocado Poulette

1 *Cook fillets, dusted with flour, in oil*

2 *Place fillets on pastry, spread with mustard, top with avocado*

FILO AVOCADO CHICKEN

Although it has been used in Middle Eastern countries for many years, filo pastry is only now becoming a common household item. It can be used with any filling, and this one is especially easy and tasty.

2 teaspoons dried tarragon
2 teaspoons French mustard
salt and freshly ground pepper
6 chicken fillets or 3 whole chicken breasts with
*   bones removed*
plain flour
2 tablespoons oil
200 g filo pastry sheets
melted butter for brushing pastry
3 avocados, thinly sliced

Mix tarragon, mustard and seasonings together. Dust chicken fillets with flour and cook in oil until nicely browned on both sides. Cool.

Using 2 sheets of filo pastry for each person, brush one sheet with melted butter, cover with second sheet and brush again. Fold in half and brush again.

Place one fillet in centre at the end of the pastry, spread over a little tarragon mustard, then top with avocado slices. Fold slices of pastry over the chicken to completely enclose. Repeat with remaining chicken.

Place on greased oven tray, brush pastry tops with butter and bake at 200°C (400°F) for 10 minutes, reducing heat to 180°C (350°F) for a further 10 to 15 minutes. Filo rolls should be a light golden brown. Serve with seasonal vegetables.

Note: you can prepare this dish up to two hours before serving time if it is kept in the refrigerator; heat for 10 minutes before serving.

Serves 6

Filo Avocado Chicken

CHICKEN AND AVOCADO PIE BECHAMEL

3 Fold over pastry

PASTRY

2 cups plain flour
125 g softened butter
½ cup cream

FILLING

2 kg chicken
6 cups water
2 leeks or onions
2 bay leaves
3 sprigs parsley
8 peppercorns
4 cloves garlic
1 teaspoon salt
3 avocados, chopped

To make pastry, cut butter into flour with knife and then rub in with fingertips until mixture resembles bread-crumbs. Mix cream in with a spoon, adding a little more if your flour absorbs more liquid.

Form dough into ball and refrigerate (in summer) for 1 hour before using; in winter, covered at room temperature for 1 hour.

Grease round pie dish and line with half of pastry.

To make filling, place whole chicken and rest of ingredients in large saucepan. Bring to the boil, cover and simmer over low heat for about 1¼ hours or until chicken is tender. Remove chicken from liquid and cool. Reserve stock.

Chop chicken into long pieces and toss with Bechamel Sauce and chopped avocado.

Add filling and top with remainder of pastry.

Glaze top of pie with a beaten egg or a little milk and bake at 200°C (400°F) for 20 to 30 minutes or until golden brown on top.

BECHAMEL SAUCE

60 g butter
50 g plain flour
300 mL cream
450 mL reserved stock
1 teaspoon tarragon
½ cup chopped parsley
salt and pepper

To make sauce, melt butter in heavy saucepan. Add flour and stir well. Remove from heat and gradually stir in stock and tarragon. Return to heat and cook, stirring, till mixture thickens.

Add cream and stir again till mixture is a very thick sauce. Add salt, pepper and parsley.

Serves 6–8

AVOCADO FRITTATA

This Italian-style open omelette is a delicious light dinner, served with a salad. You can vary the toppings but always make sure that, whichever you choose, they cover the avocado before it goes under the grill.

3 eggs
pinch of salt
pinch of cracked black pepper
2 heaped teaspoons fresh chopped herbs (marjoram,
*   thyme, basil, oregano or chervil)*
1 teaspoon olive oil
½ large avocado, sliced
¼ cup grated Parmesan cheese

Whisk the eggs until just combined, taking care not to over-beat. Stir in the salt, pepper and 1 teaspoon of the herbs. Heat the oil in a small frying pan (16 cm wide, if you have one) then reduce the temperature and add the egg mixture. Tilt the pan as the frittata sets and allow the egg mixture to run underneath.

As the frittata starts to set, lay the avocado slices over the top, sprinkle with the remaining herbs and top with grated cheese (making sure all the avocado is covered). Place under a hot grill for 1–2 minutes, or until the cheese has lightly browned and the frittata puffed. Loosen the edges with a spatula and slide onto a serving plate.

Serves 1 (or 2 as a light meal)

Avocado Frittata

Warm Salad of Tuna, Avocado and Potato

WARM SALAD OF TUNA, AVOCADO AND POTATO

The fresh taste and different textures make this salad a joy to eat. Halve the quantities for entree servings.

500 g Pontiac potatoes, unpeeled, cut into large wedges
3 tablespoons olive oil
mixed lettuce leaves
4 small tuna steaks
4 small (or 2 large) avocados, cut into wedges
2 red onions, cut into thin rings
12 black olives
1 cup mayonnaise (or use a lemon or lime aioli)
1–2 tablespoons lemon juice
finely chopped parsley

Toss the potato wedges in 2 tablespoons of the olive oil, place on a lightly greased oven tray and bake at 220°C for 20–30 minutes, or until crisp. Leave to cool for 5 minutes before serving.

Arrange the lettuce leaves on serving plates. Heat the remaining oil in a frying pan and fry the tuna over medium heat for 1 minute each side (the fish should still be pink in the centre). Flake into bite-sized chunks.

Arrange the potatoes, tuna, avocado, onion and olives over the lettuce. Mix together the mayonnaise and lemon juice and spoon over the salad. Serve immediately, sprinkled with parsley.

Serves 4

Avocado Veal Birds in Port Wine

AVOCADO VEAL BIRDS IN PORT WINE

750 g thin veal steaks
2 tablespoons seasoned flour
80 g butter
2 onions, finely chopped
1 tablespoon cornflour
½ cup stock
¼ cup port wine
½ cup cream

STUFFING

¼ cup finely chopped shallots
1 tablespoon finely chopped parsley
1 tablespoon fresh thyme leaves
grated rind 1 lemon
1 large avocado, mashed
1 cup soft breadcrumbs

To make stuffing, mix shallots, parsley, thyme, lemon rind and mashed avocado together. Work in breadcrumbs.

Divide stuffing among steaks. Roll up and secure with a skewer or string. Coat rolls with seasoned flour.

Melt butter in a frypan and brown rolls on all sides. Remove to serving dish and keep warm.

Cook onion in remaining juices in frypan. Mix in cornflour and add stock and wine. Simmer gently for about 5 minutes, then mix in cream.

Spoon sauce over rolls and serve. Some may prefer to place rolls in the oven for 10 minutes to allow all the flavours to mingle.

Serves 6

BAKED SNAPPER WITH AVOCADO

This dish, apart from looking impressive with the whole snapper has a delicately flavoured avocado stuffing. It also can be topped with the Avocado Fish Sauce. (See recipe.)

2 whole snapper, approx.
   500 g each
20 g melted butter
2 slices bread, crumbled
2 tablespoons lemon juice
1 onion, thinly sliced

1 stalk celery, finely sliced
½ teaspoon dried thyme
salt and freshly ground
   pepper
1 egg, beaten lightly
2 avocados, finely chopped

Brush cavity of fish with melted butter. Mix crumbled bread, lemon juice, onion, celery, thyme, salt and pepper, egg and avocados together. Stuff cavity of fish with avocado stuffing and secure with skewers.

Bake at 200°C on a greased tray for 30–40 minutes or until fish flakes easily with a fork. Remove skewers before serving. Garnish with finely chopped chives.

Serves 2

DEEP SEA GREEN CASSEROLE

Any seafood can be used with this dish of avocado, broccoli, macaroni and cheese sauce.

2 cups stock
4 fish fillets
250 g broccoli florets
250 g cooked macaroni
30 g butter
2 teaspoons curry powder
3 small onions, chopped
2 tablespoons flour

350 mL milk
3 tablespoons fresh lemon
   thyme, finely chopped
2 avocados, cut into
   chunks
salt and freshly ground
   pepper
150 g cheese, grated

Heat 2 cups stock and poach fish fillets for 3 minutes or until just cooked. Remove with slotted spoon. Reserve stock. Lightly cook broccoli. Into a greased casserole dish spread cooked macaroni. Cut fish into 2.5 cm pieces.

Melt butter and cook curry powder and chopped onion. Add flour. Remove from heat and add warmed milk and ¾ cup reserved stock and mix until smooth. Return to heat and thicken. Add fish, lemon thyme, salt and pepper to taste. Mix in cooked broccoli and avocado chunks. Spoon over macaroni, sprinkle over cheese and bake in hot oven for 20 minutes or until browned on top.

Serves 4–6

Deep Sea Green Casserole

SEAFOOD AVOCADO MILLE-FEUILLE

500 g puff pastry
2 medium-sized fish fillets, sea perch is very
    suitable
40 g butter
4 cooked king prawns
2 avocados, chopped and tossed with juice of
    1 lemon
2 cups Bechamel Sauce (see recipe)
fresh dill sprig to garnish

Roll out pastry and cut into 4 equal squares or rectangles. Bake in 200°C (400°F) oven for 20 minutes or until golden brown. Cut a little slit in top and cool on wire rack.

Fry fish fillets in a little butter until cooked. Break neatly into pieces.

Mix cooked fish, cooked prawns and chopped lemon avocado into bechamel sauce and very gently heat until filling is well warmed.

This filling is best heated in a frying pan, so that it does not have to be stirred quite as much.

To serve, cut cooked pastry squares in half. The inside pastry can be scooped out to give a neater effect, but many prefer it whole.

Spoon in the seafood avocado filling and replace the lid if desired. Decorate with a little filling around the edge of the puff pastry case and then garnish with the dill sprig.

Note: Nothing more than a light salad needs to be served with this dish.

Serves 4

Seafood Avocado Mille-Feuille

BOMBAY AVOCADO SCALLOPS

Mildly flavoured with Indian spices, this is an unusual treatment of avocados but very, very enjoyable.

4 avocados, halved
350 g scallops, halved
30 g butter
2 onions, finely sliced
1 Granny Smith apple, chopped small
½ teaspoon cumin
½ teaspoon coriander
½ teaspoon turmeric
1 tablespoon white wine
½ cup cream

Remove flesh from avocado, leaving shells intact. Either scoop it out with a teaspoon or make horizontal and vertical cuts in flesh without penetrating skin, then ease flesh out with a round bladed knife. Mix halved scallops with avocado flesh.

Melt butter and saute onion, apple and spices for 10 minutes, stirring often. Stir in the white wine and cream and cook further 10 minutes to reduce and thicken. Lastly, add avocado and scallops and heat gently until all ingredients are hot.

Serve by spooning back into avocado shells, with an accompaniment of rice and a cucumber salad or other salad of your choice.

Serves 4

BARRAMUNDI AND AVOCADO PROVENCALE

Barramundi is one of Australia's prize fish, but if it is not available you can use any other meaty white fish in its place. The orange-scented tomato sauce will take you on a culinary daydream to the Mediterranean.

6 barramundi fillets
30 g black olive paste
1½ avocados
1 egg white, lightly beaten
1 cup crumbled Fetta cheese
salt and freshly cracked black pepper

Preheat the oven to 200°C. Put the fish in a lightly greased, shallow baking dish. Spread the olive paste over the top of the fish. Slice the avocados and arrange over the fish fillets. Brush the surface of the avocado with egg white. Sprinkle Fetta over the top, then sprinkle with a little salt and black pepper. Bake for 5–10 minutes, depending on the thickness of your fish fillets.

Serve with Sauce Provencale and scatter with a few torn basil leaves to garnish.

SAUCE PROVENCALE

1 large onion, finely chopped
2 tablespoons olive oil
2 cloves garlic, crushed
1 bay leaf
6 large tomatoes, peeled and pureed
1 tablespoon tomato paste
rind of 1 orange, peeled into wide strips with a potato
    peeler
1 cup fish stock or water
salt and freshly cracked black pepper
3 tablespoons balsamic vinegar (or white wine)

Fry the onion in the olive oil over medium heat until soft. Add the garlic and bay leaf and fry, stirring, for a further 2 minutes. Add the tomatoes, tomato paste, orange rind and stock or water. If you are using wine instead of balsamic vinegar, add it now. Bring to the boil, stirring occasionally, then reduce the heat and simmer for 30 minutes. Season to taste with salt and pepper and add the vinegar. Simmer for a further 5 minutes. Remove the bay leaf and orange rind to serve.

Serves 6

SPINACH AVOCADO PARCELS

250 g cottage cheese
2 tablespoons chopped fresh mint
2 tablespoons chopped parsley
1 large onion, sauteed in a little butter with ½
    teaspoon sweet paprika
1 cup cooked brown rice
2 avocados, diced
8 large spinach leaves, stems carefully removed

Mix cottage cheese, mint, parsley, sauteed onion and rice. Add avocado. Place equal amounts of filling in centre of each spinach leaf and roll up securely, ensuring edges are folded in.

(Spinach may be put into really hot water for a few minutes to soften it slightly. Drain well before use.)

Steam spinach parcels in a vegetable steamer or Chinese bamboo steamer for a few minutes to allow filling to heat through and spinach to soften.

Serve with a little butter rubbed over the top, with your favourite cheese sauce or fresh Tomato Herb Sauce. See Avocado Gnocchi recipe.

Serves 4

TAGLIATELLE AVOCADO

The pasta, with its varying colours, looks delightful accompanying the avocado, and makes for an easy, satisfying meal served with salad.

450 g wholemeal tagliatelle noodles (half
    wholemeal and half spinach)
80 g butter
8 cloves garlic, crushed
1 cup fresh basil, chopped or 3 teaspoons dried basil
4 avocados, diced
½ cup chopped parsley
salt and freshly ground pepper
grated Parmesan cheese (optional)

Cook noodles as directed. Drain and set aside. Melt butter in large saucepan, adding garlic and basil. Saute 5 minutes.

Add cooked noodles, avocado, parsley and seasonings and toss gently until all ingredients are heated through.

To serve, sprinkle on cheese if desired.

Serves 4

Barramundi and Avocado Provencale

CRUSTY STUFFED AVOCADO

CRUST

½ cup dry breadcrumbs
½ cup sesame seeds
1 teaspoon caraway seeds
2 eggs, beaten well
plain flour

FILLING

2 medium-sized avocados
juice 1 lemon
125 g Camembert cheese, chopped small
1 clove garlic, crushed
3 tablespoons finely chopped fresh herbs
dash or two Tabasco sauce
freshly ground pepper

Combine breadcrumbs, sesame seeds and caraway seeds. Have ready in deep, wide bowl to coat avocado. Do the same for the flour and beaten eggs.

To make filling, cut avocados in half lengthways. Scoop out seed and a little of flesh. Mash flesh with cheese, garlic, herbs, Tabasco and pepper.

Pour a little lemon juice into avocado shells and put mashed filling back in. Put avocado together again and carefully peel skin away.

Coat whole avocado in flour, then beaten egg, then crumb mixture. Repeat coating process once again.

Fry in hot oil until golden brown (to seal), then bake at about 200°C (400°F) in oven dish until heated through (about 15 minutes). Top with Almond Butter Sauce.

Note: After frying avocado in oil, it may be refrigerated for a while before baking, and then heated in the oven.

ALMOND BUTTER SAUCE

60 g butter
1 teaspoon sweet paprika
2 tablespoons slivered, roasted almonds
juice ¼ lemon

Melt butter and add paprika. Cook for a few minutes then add nuts and lemon juice.

Serves 2

CORN AND AVOCADO TACOS

Tacos, using this delicious avocado-based filling, make a perfect lunch or light dinner.

30 g butter
2 medium-sized onions, finely chopped
2 cloves garlic, crushed
½ teaspoon dried basil
corn kernels, scraped from 3 cobs or 1 small can
    corn kernels
1 cup cooked red kidney beans
3 small avocados, chopped
1 cup grated cheese
1 cup sour cream
paprika and a tomato, for the garnish

Melt butter in a frypan. Cook onions, garlic and basil for 5 minutes over a moderate heat. Add corn and cook further 5 minutes. Toss through cooked kidney beans until hot and then arrange the chopped avocado over the mixture. Place lid on frypan and turn off heat. Leave for a few minutes, to allow avocado to warm. Toss mixture gently and fill each taco just over half way, topping with grated cheese and some sour cream. Sprinkle paprika over sour cream and garnish with a tomato slice when serving.

Serves 4–6

POTATO AND AVOCADO CROQUETTES

This is a good way to use up left-over potatoes and an adequate meal to serve for a light dinner or lunch, even as a side dish.

2 large potatoes, scrubbed and coarsely chopped
20 g butter
2 tablespoons chopped Fetta cheese
2 medium-sized avocados, chopped small
1 egg, beaten well
½ cup chopped parsley
6 green or black olives, chopped small
freshly ground pepper
2 eggs, beaten with 1 tablespoon water
breadcrumbs for coating
oil for frying

Cook potatoes until tender. Mash with butter. Cool.

Add Fetta cheese, avocados, egg, parsley, olives and pepper to cooled mashed potato. Form into sausage shaped croquettes. Roll in egg beaten with water, then breadcrumbs. Fry in shallow oil on all sides until golden brown.

Note: Croquettes are delicious dipped in tartare sauce or mayonnaise.

Serves 3–4

Crusty Stuffed Avocado

1 *Mash prepared avocado with cheese, garlic, herbs, Tabasco and pepper*

2 *Pile filling into avocado*

3 *Coat avocado with beaten egg and flour*

CHICKEN AVOCADO CROQUETTES

A crisp coating covers this creamy smooth centre of chicken, egg, avocado and herb sauce. A mouthwatering meal for lunch or dinner.

2 cups finely chopped,
    cooked chicken
2 avocados, cut into small
    pieces
2 hard-boiled eggs,
    chopped
1 tablespoon lemon juice
⅔ cup flour
2 eggs, beaten
⅔ cup breadcrumbs
oil for deep-frying

HERB SAUCE

80 g butter
4 shallots, finely chopped
4 tablespoons plain flour
3 teaspoons Dijon mustard
1 cup milk
2 tablespoons fresh herbs
    (parsley, thyme or basil)
salt and freshly ground
    pepper

To make Herb Sauce, melt butter and saute shallots for a few minutes. Remove from heat and stir in flour and mustard. Cook again for 2 minutes. Remove from heat and gradually stir in milk. Cook, stirring, until smooth and thick. Add finely chopped fresh herbs, salt and pepper.

Mix chicken, avocado and hard-boiled eggs into Herb Sauce with lemon juice. Chill mixture for a couple of hours.

Form mixture into croquette shapes and dip into beaten egg and breadcrumbs. Cook in hot oil for 5–10 minutes or until golden brown.

Makes 8 large or 24 regular croquettes

Chicken Avocado Croquettes

Summer Roll

SUMMER ROLL

60 g butter
1 large onion, sliced thinly
3 medium-sized carrots, grated
1 bunch spinach, shredded
2 avocados, chopped
1 cup mung beans or Chinese bean sprouts
3 small sprigs fresh dill or ½ teaspoon dried dill

Melt butter and saute onion and carrot for 10 minutes with lid on pan, stirring occasionally. Add spinach.

Stir well and cook further for a few minutes until spinach is soft. Cool.

Add avocados and mix well. Add sprouts and dill.

This filling can be rolled with puff pastry, wholemeal pastry, filo pastry or spring roll sheets.

Glaze pastry with milk and glaze spring roll sheets with melted butter before baking.

Place filled rolls on greased tray and cook at 220°C (425°F) until lightly browned.

SPRING ROLL

1 cup water
1 cup plain flour
1 egg
1 tablespoon oil

Blend ingredients in blender until smooth, adding more water if too thick. This batter should be of a similar consistency to crepe batter, allowing for it to thicken as it stands. Leave in refrigerator for 30 minutes.

Heat frypan; when hot turn down to a low heat. Pour batter over pan, tilting so as to move it evenly and thinly over surface.

Cook until batter comes away easily; cook other side 1 minute. These should not be browned at all, like crepes.

Note: The unfilled spring roll sheets freeze well, separated with plastic and cooled completely beforehand. They can also be deep-fried in oil, if preferred to baking.

Serves 6

BROCCOLI AVOCADO LORRAINE

250 g broccoli
2 avocados, sliced
1½ cups cream
1 teaspoon dry mustard
2 pinches nutmeg
5 eggs
1 cup grated cheese
freshly ground pepper

Separate broccoli into small florets and cook until only just tender. Grease a pie dish with butter and arrange cooked broccoli and avocado in layers.

Beat together or blend the cream, mustard, nutmeg and eggs. Pour over vegetables and top with grated cheese and freshly ground pepper.

Bake at 180°C (350°F) for about 30 minutes until set and lightly browned on top.

Note: A white sauce with lots of chopped parsley goes well with this dish.

Serves 6

GUANAJUATO AVOCADO OMELETTE

1 large avocado, chopped
2 tablespoons sour cream
1 tablespoon lemon juice
½ cup grated Mozzarella cheese
60 g butter
salt and freshly ground pepper
4 large eggs, beaten well

Toss avocado, sour cream, lemon juice and cheese in a bowl. Set aside.

Melt butter in a frying pan and evenly coat the pan with it. When butter is foaming, let it subside. Whip salt and pepper through beaten eggs. Pour in beaten eggs and tilt pan so they spread evenly. When omelette starts to set, loosen edges and carefully lift them, tilting pan so the uncooked eggs run to the bottom.

Spoon avocado filling onto one half of the omelette and fold over the other half. Cook over a low heat for about 3 minutes on each side. Serve topped with Chilli Sauce if desired.

CHILLI SAUCE

1 large tomato, finely chopped
1 tablespoon tomato paste
1 tablespoon fresh chillies, very finely chopped
2 tablespoons grated onion
1 tablespoon cider vinegar
1 clove garlic, crushed

Mix all ingredients together and cook for approximately 30 minutes, until thick.

Serves 2

Broccoli Avocado Lorraine

RICOTTA AVOCADO FLAN

The flavours in this flan are similar to a pizza. This recipe makes a very nutritious meal with the addition of a leafy salad.

PASTRY

200 g plain flour
100 g soft butter
juice ½ lemon
¼ cup water

FILLING

500 g ricotta cheese
3 large eggs, beaten
pinch nutmeg
1 large onion, chopped
1 capsicum, finely chopped
2 zucchini, grated
40 g butter
¼ cup fresh basil or 1 teaspoon dried basil
2 tomatoes, chopped
2 tablespoons tomato paste
3 avocados, sliced
2 cups grated cheese

To make filling, beat ricotta with eggs and nutmeg. Cook onion, capsicum and zucchini in butter for 10 minutes. Then add basil, tomatoes and tomato paste and cook until tomatoes are well cooked and mixture is of a sauce-like consistency.

To assemble, roll out pastry and line a greased pie dish with it. Put a thin layer of ricotta mixture over the bottom of the pastry, then a layer of the tomato and vegetable mixture, followed by a layer of avocado slices and, lastly, a layer of grated cheese.

Repeat all the layers again if you have the room, ending with grated cheese.

Bake at 180°C (350°F) for about 30 minutes.

Note: You can serve this flan hot or at room temperature.

Serves 8–10

SCOTTISH SALMON AND AVOCADO PIE

PASTRY

1 cup plain flour
1 cup rolled oats
125 g butter, softened
1 cup grated cheese
water

FILLING

1 cup cooked rice
220 g salmon
2 medium-sized avocados,
*   chopped*

½ cup sour cream
1 small onion, chopped
2 tomatoes, chopped
3 eggs, beaten slightly
1 tablespoon lemon juice
2 tablespoons chopped
*   parsley*

Combine flour and oats in a bowl. Rub in small bits of the softened butter until mixture resembles coarse breadcrumbs. Toss cheese through and add a little water to make a soft dough. Stand for 30 minutes, covered, before using.

To make filling, toss together rice, salmon, avocados, sour cream, onion, tomatoes, beaten eggs, lemon juice and parsley.

Grease a pie dish or oval casserole dish.

Roll out just over half of pastry on floured surface and fit into bottom of pie dish. Spoon in filling. Roll out remaining pastry to cover top of pie and seal edges together well by pinching them against the sides of the pie dish. Put a small slit in the middle of the pastry to allow steam to escape during cooking.

Glaze the top with a little milk and bake in a moderate oven 180°C (350°F) for 30 minutes.

Note: This pastry is rolled a little thicker than normal shortcrust pastry, as you will notice when rolling it out to fit the pie or casserole dish.   Serves 8

AVOCADO PASTY

pastry sheets cut into 15 cm rounds

FILLING

cubed avocado tossed with a little lemon juice
salt and freshly ground pepper

This avocado filling can be used with any pastry (shortcrust, puff or flaky). Simply cut pastry into 15 cm rounds, place filling on one half. Moisten edges and fold over to form a half-moon shape. Press edges together well.

Place on greased tray, brush with a little milk and bake at 200°C (400°F) until lightly browned.

Note: A tasty addition is the sprinkling of cheese over the filling before the pastry is sealed down.   Serves 4

Scottish Salmon and Avocado Pie

WALNUT AND AVOCADO ROULADE

60 g butter
⅓ cup plain flour
1 cup milk
1 teaspoon French mustard
⅔ cup grated cheese
4 eggs, separated
250 g cooked spinach (optional)

FILLING

3 avocados, chopped
⅔ cup walnut pieces
½ cup chopped parsley
6 shallots, chopped
½ cup freshly grated Parmesan cheese

Melt butter and stir in flour until smooth. Cook 1 minute and remove from heat. Gradually add milk and cook over moderate heat, stirring, until thick.

Remove and add mustard and cheese. 250 g cooked spinach (with all moisture squeezed out) can be mixed in at this stage for variety.

Mix well. Stir in egg yolks one at a time. Beat whites until soft peaks form and gently fold into cheese sauce with a metal spoon. Don't over-mix.

Pour into greased 30 x 25 cm lamington tin lined with greaseproof paper. Bake in moderate oven for 15 minutes or until puffed and lightly browned. (If pressed gently with finger, roulade should bounce into shape again.)

Turn out onto a tea towel. Peel paper off carefully and gently roll up with the aid of the towel. Leave for 5 minutes and then unroll.

Spread with filling (combine all ingredients and mix well), not quite covering one end so that mixture will not come out. Roll up.

Put onto tray again and sprinkle with Parmesan. Garnish top with walnut halves and heat at high temperature for about 15 minutes.

Serves 6

1 *Pour into a greased and lined lamington tin*

Walnut and Avocado Roulade

2 *Spread filling, not quite covering one end*

3 *Roll and place in tray again*

BERNOISE SPINACH AND AVOCADO LOAF

½ loaf fresh bread
milk to soak
4 eggs, separated
¼ cup chopped fresh dill
pinch or two nutmeg
2 bunches spinach, shredded
handful fresh mint leaves
250 g butter
250 g cream cheese
3 avocados, mashed with a little lemon juice

Soak bread in sufficient milk to make bread moist.

Mix soaked bread with beaten egg yolks, dill and nutmeg.

Saute spinach and mint in butter until soft. Add chopped cream cheese and mix through until it starts to melt.

Puree spinach mixture in blender until smooth. Mix with soaked bread and avocados. Consistency of final mixture should be soft but not sloppy. If too moist add small amount of dry breadcrumbs.

Beat egg whites until soft peaks form; fold gently through spinach mixture.

Pour into greased 30 x 20 cm dish and bake at 180°C (350°F) for about 30 minutes or until puffed and lightly browned.

Note: The loaf can be served on its own, with a spoonful of sour cream or a mushroom sauce. Garnish with dill.

Serves 8–10

Bernoise Spinach and Avocado Loaf

CAMEMBERT AVOCADO CAKE

1 whole Camembert
1 avocado, thinly sliced
flour (to coat)
1 beaten egg

breadcrumbs (to coat)
oil to deep-fry or butter to
    shallow fry

Slice a very firm Camembert in three even layers. Between each layer, place overlapping slices of avocado. Form whole Camembert into a firm round.

Dip in flour, then beaten egg, then breadcrumbs and repeat coating process once again to form a thick crust.

Heat oil or butter. Cook whole Camembert cake on both sides until golden brown. During cooking, use an egg slice and the back of a spoon to gently hold the rounded edge of the Camembert cake in place while turning gently.

Top with small diced carrots cooked in a little butter and honey with a pinch of cinnamon.

Serves 2

SAVOURY CREPE BATTER

This batter recipe is basic for all main meal crepes; it will make about 10 crepes.

2 eggs
2 cups milk
⅔ cup plain flour
2 tablespoons oil
optional: 2 tablespoons ground roasted sesame
    seeds
1 teaspoon sweet paprika or 1 teaspoon of your
    favourite herb

Blend all ingredients in a blender. Turn machine off, stir down flour and blend again. Refrigerate 1 hour before using.

HAM, CHEESE AND AVOCADO CREPES

If you have ready-made crepes on hand, this is a very quick meal to prepare.

6 prepared crepes (see Savoury Crepe Batter)
6 thickly sliced pieces of ham (enough to cover ½
    of each crepe)
3 avocados, thinly sliced
Edam cheese (enough to cover ½ of each crepe)

On half of each crepe place ham, avocado and then cheese. Fold crepe over. Gently heat a little butter in a crepe pan or frying pan and cook each crepe on both sides until outside is slightly crisp and browned and filling is hot.

Serves 6

CAMEMBERT AVOCADO CREPE WITH CAPER SAUCE

3 avocados, thinly sliced
3 whole Camembert cheeses, sliced
6 prepared crepes

SAUCE

60 g butter
60 g plain flour
150 mL stock
2 tablespoons tamari or soy sauce
150 mL white wine
150 mL cream
3 tablespoons capers (rinsed under running water to
    remove the excess salt and dried with a paper towel)

Lay avocado slices over half of crepe. Then add Camembert slices. Fold and brown on both sides in a little butter.

Melt butter in saucepan. Add flour to make a roux. Cook for a few minutes to brown lightly. Remove from heat and slowly add stock while stirring. Add tamari and white wine.

Cook over medium heat, stirring occasionally, then add cream and capers. Cook until reasonably thick and spoon over filled, cooked crepes.

Garnish with a sprig of parsley and a sprinkling of capers.

Serves 6

ASPARAGUS AVOCADO CREPE

Fresh asparagus is almost a must for this recipe, however the tinned variety may be used as a last resort.

18 medium-sized asparagus stalks
6 cooked crepes
125 g Swiss cheese, grated
3 avocados, sliced thinly

Trim woody ends from asparagus and cook in boiling water for about 10 minutes or in a vegetable steamer until the stalks are tender. Drain well.

Arrange, on one half of each crepe, grated cheese, then avocado slices, then asparagus stalks.

Fold over top half and cook each side over moderate heat until insides are heated and outside of crepe is lightly crisped.

Serves 6

PRAWN AND AVOCADO CREPE

40 g butter
1 capsicum, sliced
1 onion, sliced
2 cloves garlic, crushed
1 cup thick tomato sauce
dash Tabasco sauce
500 g peeled, cooked prawns
150 mL cream
4 cooked crepes
2 tomatoes, sliced
4 avocados, pureed

Melt butter and cook capsicum, onion and garlic until tender. Stir in tomato sauce and Tabasco sauce and cook for a few minutes. Add prawns and cream and cook until heated through.

Spoon into cooked crepes and serve garnished with tomato slices topped with avocado puree.

Serves 4

ALFALFA AVOCADO CREPE

250 g cottage cheese
4 tablespoons finely shredded shallots
8 cooked crepes
2 avocados, sliced
2 loosely packed cups alfalfa sprouts
20 g butter
lemon juice

Combine cottage cheese and shallots. Spread over one half of cooked crepe. Top with avocado slices and alfalfa sprouts. Fold crepe over filling and cook gently in a little butter until filling is heated and crepe is lightly browned and crisp on both sides.

Sprinkle a little lemon juice over when serving.

Serves 4

Fillings for Crepes: Alfalfa Avocado (top)
Prawn and Avocado (centre) Oriental Cashew (bottom)

52

ORIENTAL CASHEW CREPE

A light crepe meal enhanced with subtle flavours of the Orient.

3 tablespoons oil
2 cups raw chicken strips
½ cup thinly sliced broccoli
1 onion, finely sliced
1½ cups chicken stock
2 tablespoons grated fresh root ginger
⅔ cup roasted, chopped cashew nuts
½ cup finely shredded shallots
2 tablespoons arrowroot or cornflour
2 tablespoons tamari or soy sauce
2 large avocados, finely diced
12 cooked crepes
6 shallot curls
1 avocado half, sliced (for garnish)

Heat oil in frypan. Add chicken strips and sliced broccoli and gently toss for about 5 minutes. Add onion and stock with ginger. Cover and simmer for 10 minutes.

Remove chicken and broccoli and toss with cashew nuts and shallots.

Dissolve arrowroot or cornflour in tamari and stir into stock mixture. Cook, stirring over medium heat until thick. Set aside.

To serve, mix diced avocado with chicken filling and put into centre of each crepe. Roll up and cook gently over medium heat in a little butter in frypan on both sides.

Spoon over sauce and top with a shallot curl and an avocado slice.

Serves 6

LEBANESE AVOCADO CAULIFLOWER

1 medium-sized cauliflower
1 clove garlic
½ teaspoon salt
½ cup lemon juice
1 cup tahini paste
2 avocados, chopped
1 cup water or stock
½ cup roasted pine nuts
  and ½ cup chopped
  parsley

Steam or boil whole cauliflower in large saucepan till tender.

Blend (in blender) garlic, salt and lemon juice until a smooth puree. Then add tahini paste, chopped avocados and enough water or stock to make a reasonably thick sauce.

Gently warm the sauce in a saucepan until hot and pour over whole hot cauliflower placed on a serving platter.

Garnish with roasted pine nuts and chopped parsley and place in centre of dinner table for an impressive dish.

Serves 4

LEEK AND AVOCADO CRUNCH

1 large brown onion, thinly sliced
4 good-sized leeks, well washed and thinly sliced
½ cup white wine
2 tablespoons tamari or 1 tablespoon soya sauce
2 medium-sized avocados, well mashed
juice ½ lemon
150 g blue vein cheese
1 cup Swiss cheese, grated

CRUNCH

1 cup plain flour
½ cup rolled oats
2 tablespoons toasted sesame seeds
½ cup walnuts, coarsely chopped
1 teaspoon sweet paprika
½ cup melted butter

Grease a deep baking dish with a little butter. Place sliced onion and leeks in layers and pour over the white wine and tamari. Cover with foil and bake at 180°C (350°F) for 40 minutes. Remove from oven.

Mix mashed avocado with the lemon juice and blue vein cheese. Spread over cooked onions and leeks and top with grated cheese. Combine all of the crunch ingredients in a bowl and mix well. Spoon onto leek mixture evenly and bake at 190°C (375°F) for 15 minutes or until lightly browned on top.

Serves 8

GARDEN AVOCADO MORNAY

A melt-in-the-mouth mornay to eat with a light salad. Any combination of vegetables can be used.

2 chopped avocados
1 large potato, cooked and sliced
2 cobs corn, cooked and scraped or ½ small can of
  corn kernels
½ cup chopped cooked pumpkin
½ cup fresh peas, cooked
parsley to garnish

Toss with prepared Mornay Sauce and serve immediately or put into greased baking dish and heat through in oven until lightly browned on top.

MORNAY SAUCE

3 cups milk
1 small onion, sliced
3 bay leaves
1 teaspoon whole dried thyme
100 g butter
½ cup plain flour
⅔ cup grated cheese
½ cup grated Parmesan cheese
freshly ground pepper
pinch nutmeg

Infuse milk with onion, bay leaves and thyme over moderate heat. Don't boil.

Remove from heat and stand for 15 minutes with a lid on. Strain. Melt butter and stir in flour to form a roux. Cook 3 minutes. Remove from heat and slowly stir in strained milk.

Mix until smooth and return to heat, stirring until sauce thickens. Beat with rotary beater to smooth sauce out. Add cheeses and stir until melted. Season to taste with pepper and nutmeg.

Serves 4

Lebanese Avocado Cauliflower

SALADS, SNACKS AND OTHER SURPRISES

Avocado goes well with virtually any salad combination — and in this chapter there are some special ones. The pale yellow-green of the avocado complements the contrasting colours of other fruits and vegetables and makes arranging an avocado salad a joy.
Not all sauces appear in this section, as some follow related individual recipes throughout the book. A sweet avocado sauce is tasty to eat and a visual delight when served with a fruit salad, and the savoury avocado sauces are particularly good with seafood.
As well as a range of snacks there are some unusual drink combinations — perfect for a nourishing breakfast, a lunch when time is short or a refreshing break at any time of day.
Sweet and savoury recipes using avocados provide easily digestible and highly nutritious meals for babies and will also be enjoyed by older children.

AVOCADO CREAM SAUCE

Delicious served over a salad of luscious tropical fruits.

1 avocado
2 teaspoons honey
300 mL cream

Blend all ingredients until smooth and thick in a blender or food processor.
   Note: Weight-conscious people can substitute cottage cheese or natural yoghurt for the cream.

Serves 2

AVOCADO FISH SAUCE

Enhances crumbed fish fillets or grilled fish.

1 clove garlic, crushed
1 tablespoon butter
1 large avocado, mashed
100 mL cream
2 teaspoons lemon juice

Cook crushed garlic in butter for a few minutes, stirring, until golden brown. Stir in mashed avocado, cream and lemon juice and heat through. Don't allow to boil.
   Note: You can reheat this sauce within a period of about two hours.

Serves 2

Avocado Cream Sauce

AVOCADO SALAD DRESSING

2 egg yolks
¼ cup lemon juice
½ teaspoon salt
½ teaspoon freshly ground pepper
1 tablespoon wine vinegar or apple cider vinegar
1 tablespoon chopped onion
1 avocado
½ cup salad oil

Blend egg yolks, lemon juice, salt and pepper, vinegar and onion. Then add avocado while blender is in motion.
   Add oil slowly until thick, like mayonnaise. If all of the oil can't be added, add a little water and then the remaining oil.
   Your favourite herbs can be added to this dressing (chives, tarragon, parsley, dill or basil go very well). These quantities should yield 1½ cups of dressing.

ALLIGATOR PEAR FRUIT SAUCE

Alligator Pear was the original name for the avocado.

1 avocado
1 dessertspoon honey
juice 1 orange

Blend all ingredients in a blender until smooth. Cream can be folded through this or a banana can be added.
   Note: Serve this recipe over fruit salad tossed in coconut.

Serves 2

EGG AND AVOCADO SAUCE

A creamy egg sauce, delightful with pasta.

2 cups milk
1 large avocado, chopped
50 g butter
2 tablespoons plain flour
½ teaspoon prepared mustard
salt and freshly ground pepper
2 hard-boiled eggs, chopped
3 tablespoons finely chopped chives

Blend milk with avocado until smooth. Melt butter and stir in flour, mustard and seasonings. Add avocado milk and stir constantly until sauce thickens. Reduce heat and simmer for a few minutes, adding chopped eggs and chives.

Note: Tuna complements this sauce well; 150 g can tuna can be added with the eggs and chives. If serving with pasta, sprinkle some grated parmesan cheese on top.

Serves 4

Orange Dressing

SCALLOP AND AVOCADO SALAD

500 g scallops
1½ cups fresh orange juice
2 large avocados, cut into thick slices
½ red capsicum, sliced thinly
½ green capsicum, sliced thinly
1 orange, segmented and skinned for garnish

ORANGE DRESSING

½ cup reduced orange juice
pinch or two sweet paprika
salt and freshly ground pepper
1 tablespoon wine vinegar
¼ cup olive oil

Cut scallops in half and place in saucepan with orange juice. Bring to the boil, lower heat and simmer for 12 minutes. Remove scallops with a slotted spoon. Bring juice back to the boil and reduce to about ½ cup in quantity for use in dressing. Cool.

Combine all dressing ingredients.

Marinate scallops in dressing for 1 hour before serving. To serve salad, spoon marinated scallops onto a platter and decorate with avocado slices and capsicum slices. Pour a little more dressing over salad and serve garnished with fresh orange segments around edge of platter.

Serves 4   *Scallop and Avocado Salad*

ISRAELI AVOCADO

2 avocados, halved, peeled and sliced lengthways
2 oranges, peeled and in segments
8 strawberries
fresh mint leaves

DRESSING

250 g cream cheese   2 dessertspoons honey
juice 2 lemons   about ½ cup oil
handful fresh mint leaves

Arrange alternate slices of avocado and orange on a plate or use your own imaginative presentation.

Garnish with strawberries and fresh mint leaves and serve dressing separately in a bowl or jug.

To make dressing, combine all ingredients in a bowl and mix well.

Serves 4

GRAPE AVOCADO SALAD

2 large avocados, shaped into balls with a melon
    baller
2 cups green grapes, seeded
2 shallots, chopped
1 medium-sized lettuce, torn into pieces
½ large cucumber, peeled and chopped
3 radishes, thinly sliced
2 tomatoes sliced and cut in quarters

Toss all ingredients with your own French dressing, and serve.

Serves 6–8

Red Wine Vinegar Dressing

Spiral Pasta and Avocado Salad

SPIRAL PASTA AND AVOCADO SALAD

250 g cooked spiral pasta   2 large tomatoes, chopped
2 avocados, chopped   4 shallots, chopped
½ cup finely chopped   ¼ cup finely chopped
    fresh basil   parsley
1 dessertspoon capers

Toss all ingredients together with prepared dressing and serve.

RED WINE VINEGAR DRESSING

¼–½ cup olive oil
⅓ cup red wine vinegar
1 heaped teaspoon tomato
    paste
2 tablespoons chives,
    chopped
salt and freshly ground
    pepper

Combine in a jar and shake well.

Serves 6

POTATO AVOCADO SALAD WITH HORSERADISH DRESSING

An unusual change from the plain old-fashioned potato salad we are all familiar with.

400 g potatoes, cooked whole, peeled when cool
    and cut into chunks
small bunch shallots, finely chopped
2 red skinned apples, cut into small pieces
3 avocados, cut into chunks
walnuts or pecans, chopped for garnish
parsley, chopped for garnish

Place all ingredients, except avocados, nuts and parsley in a bowl. Toss with horseradish dressing and, lastly, add chopped avocado carefully.
    Garnish salad with chopped walnuts or pecans and parsley.

HORSERADISH DRESSING

1 cup sour cream
3 teaspoons horseradish cream
3 teaspoons lemon juice
salt and freshly ground pepper

Combine all ingredients and pour over salad.

Serves 6

Egg, Avocado and Beet Salad

Horseradish Dressing

EGG, AVOCADO AND BEET SALAD

500 g cooked beetroot, thinly sliced into julienne
    strips
2 avocados, finely sliced
4 hard-boiled eggs, chopped carefully into chunks
fresh dill to garnish (optional)

Arrange beetroot strips on a plate, avocado on top and chopped egg on top of that. Spoon over dressing.
    Note: Reserve a little of the cooked egg white which can be very finely chopped and sprinkled over the finished salad. Garnish with fresh dill if desired.

DRESSING

1 tablespoon French mustard
3 tablespoons wine vinegar
½ cup olive oil
salt and freshly ground pepper
1 tablespoon finely chopped onion

Combine all ingredients in a bowl and beat with a fork or whisk until well mixed.

Serves 4

Potato Avocado Salad with Horseradish Dressing

Tropical Mango and Avocado Salad

TROPICAL MANGO AND AVOCADO SALAD

2 avocados, cut into slices
  lengthways
2 mangoes, cut same as
  avocado

GARNISH

Pineapple slices
curly endive or mignonette
  lettuce
julienne strips of carrot,
  celery, capsicum,
  zucchini and cucumber
cherry tomatoes

PINEAPPLE DRESSING

100 g fresh pineapple,
  chopped
20 mL salad vinegar
1 teaspoon honey
oil

To make dressing, blend all ingredients until smooth, adding only enough oil to make a reasonably thick dressing. Taste for seasonings.

To serve, place avocado and mango slices in a fan shape on the plate. Pour over prepared dressing. Garnish plate with pineapple slices, curly endive or mignonette lettuce leaves and decorate with tropical flowers, julienne vegetables and cherry tomatoes.

Alternatively, chop mangoes and avocados into chunks, toss with dressing and serve in a hollowed out fresh pineapple half, as a centrepiece.

Serves 4–6

PRAWN AVOCADO SALAD BOWL

1 kg cooked prawns
2 avocados, formed into balls with a melon baller
2 medium-sized carrots, cut into julienne strips
2 celery stalks, cut into julienne strips
1 small Chinese cabbage, finely shredded
1 shallot, finely shredded
1 tablespoon roasted sesame seeds

Toss all ingredients together with dressing; chill for a little while before serving. Sprinkle salad with shredded shallot and sesame seeds and serve on a bed of curly endive, if desired.

DRESSING

juice 1 lemon
1 clove garlic, crushed
1 cup salad oil
½ bunch finely chopped shallots
salt and freshly ground pepper

Shake all ingredients in a jar and allow to stand for 1 hour before using.

Serves 4

MINTED ORANGE AND AVOCADO SALAD

4 slices fresh pineapple
4 lettuce or curly endive leaves
2 avocados, finely sliced or shredded
2 oranges, peeled and segmented

GARNISH

orange and chive shreds
2 tablespoons roasted chopped hazelnuts

Place pineapple slices on lettuce leaves. Arrange avocado slices and orange segments over pineapple.

Spoon over Creamy Orange Dressing and garnish with hazelnuts, and orange and chive shreds.

CREAMY ORANGE DRESSING

125 g cream cheese
juice 2 oranges, or vary to make dressing required
  thickness
a handful fresh mint

Blend cream cheese, orange juice and mint in blender until of good consistency or beat with fork until smooth. Chill before serving.

Serves 4

Minted Orange and Avocado Salad

Nordic Avocado Pear Salad

NORDIC AVOCADO PEAR SALAD

2 avocados, sliced
2 large pears (peeled only if skin isn't in good
*   condition) and finely sliced*
4 large slices Jarlsberg cheese, cut in julienne strips
4 lettuce leaves
2 tablespoons pecan nuts, halved

Arrange avocado, pear and cheese slices attractively on lettuce leaf and top with dressing. Sprinkle with a little paprika or poppy seeds to garnish and finish with a sprinkling of pecan nuts.

NORDIC DRESSING

1 tablespoon honey
1 tablespoon lemon juice
salt and freshly ground pepper
½ cup sour cream

Beat honey, lemon juice and seasonings with a fork in a bowl. Gradually beat in sour cream.

Serves 4

64

CAESAR SALAD

4–6 slices French stick (day old)
olive oil
small Cos lettuce leaves
1 large avocado, chopped
1 cup diced cooked bacon
4 tablespoons shallots, finely chopped
4 tablespoons finely sliced sun-dried tomatoes
4 tablespoons freshly grated Parmesan cheese

CAESAR DRESSING

1 egg
1 teaspoon Dijon mustard
1 clove garlic, chopped
3 anchovies, drained
3 tablespoons lemon juice or cider vinegar
70 mL light virgin olive oil
70 mL sunflower or mild vegetable oil

Slice the bread and brush each slice with oil on both sides. Cut into small cubes and place on a baking tray. Bake at 180°C for 10–15 minutes, or until the bread is hard. (Croutons can be stored in an airtight container for up to a week if necessary so you could prepare a whole loaf of French bread at one time.)

Use the lettuce leaves to line a large serving bowl or small individual bowls. Put the avocado, bacon, shallots, tomatoes and cheese in a mixing bowl. Add Caesar Dressing, toss well and then spoon over the lettuce.

To make Caesar Dressing: put the egg in a pan of cold water, bring to the boil and cook for 1 minute. Cool under running cold water for 1 minute. Shell the egg and put the white and yolk in a blender. Add the mustard, garlic, anchovies and lemon juice or vinegar and blend until smooth. Gradually add the oils, with the blender running, until the mixture thickens like mayonnaise.

Serve within 10 minutes or the salad will become soggy.

Serves 4–6

Caesar Salad

SALAD OF THE SUN

400 g fresh tuna steaks (or canned tuna if necessary)
2 tablespoons fresh orange juice
2 tablespoons balsamic or red wine vinegar
2 tablespoons virgin olive oil
pinch of salt
freshly cracked black pepper
4 spring onions, thinly sliced on the diagonal
8 black olives
8 green olives
2 large oranges, peeled and segmented
2 avocados, peeled and cut into crescents
16 cherry tomatoes
1 red capsicum, finely chopped

Sear the tuna steaks quickly on both sides in a little olive oil until cooked on the surface but still slightly pink in the middle. Flake roughly into bite-sized chunks. Put the orange juice, vinegar, oil, salt and pepper in a screw-top jar and shake to combine. Put the spring onions, olives, orange segments, avocado, tomatoes, capsicum and tuna in a salad bowl, pour over the dressing and toss gently together.

Serves 4

Salad of the Sun

1 *Cut the top off each tomato and remove pulp*

GUACAMOLE STUFFED TOMATOES

An exciting use for a well-known filling.

4 large tomatoes
2 small avocados, mashed
⅓ cup lemon juice
1 clove garlic, crushed
salt and freshly ground pepper
1 tablespoon finely chopped green chillies or pinch
  or two of chilli powder
2 tablespoons chopped parsley
½ teaspoon coriander powder
several black olives

Cut off the top of each tomato. Cut around inside edge of tomato to remove pulp from the sides, being careful not to damage the skin. Scoop out tomato pulp with a teaspoon.

Mix avocados with remaining ingredients. Beat with a fork until well mixed and smooth. Add half of the chopped tomato pulp to avocado mixture. Pile back into tomato shells. Garnish with olives.

Note: This recipe makes a superb accompaniment to most main dishes and any salad. Cherry tomatoes can be substituted for use as an hors d'oeuvre.

Serves 4

Guacamole Stuffed Tomatoes

2 *Mix avocados with remaining ingredients*

3 *Pile back into tomato shells, with a garnish of olives*

ORIENTAL STUFFED AVOCADO

The inspiration for this book. This recipe is a sentimental favourite of mine; it won an award and set me on the road to writing this book.

1 tablespoon chopped
parsley
2 tablespoons finely
chopped celery
1 tablespoon finely
shredded shallots

3 tablespoons alfalfa
sprouts or Chinese mung
bean sprouts
1 large avocado, halved
and seeded

SAUCE

1 tablespoon freshly grated
ginger
1 clove garlic, crushed

60 g tamari or soy sauce
enough honey to sweeten
to taste (about 1
tablespoon)

Toss together the parsley, celery, shallots and sprouts. Spoon this into cavity of avocado, piling high.

To make the sauce, put all ingredients in blender and blend until smooth. The flavour of the sauce improves if made the day before.

Cover avocado lightly with sauce and sprinkle with finely chopped or slivered toasted almonds.

Oriental Stuffed Avocado

Serves 2

Wined Avocado Spread

WINED AVOCADO SPREAD

A deliciously creamy spread that can be served with Melba toast or crackers after a meal, as an entree or a snack, or with a selection of crudites.

2 x 150g tins Camembert cheese
1 cup dry white wine
250 g avocados
few drops Tabasco sauce
160 g ground, lightly roasted almonds

Chop Camembert cheese coarsely and marinate with wine and Tabasco. Mash a little. Allow to stand overnight and strain the next day. The liquid remaining could be used to make a white wine sauce.

Mash Camembert with avocado until smooth and creamy (an electric mixer does this well). Refrigerate 10 minutes or so, until firm enough to mould.

This can now be placed into little pots and sprinkled with ground nuts, or moulded into empty avocado shells, and taken out carefully when very well chilled and firm.

The moulded spread can be rolled in the ground almonds.

Serves 10–12

SANDWICH TOPPINGS AND FILLINGS

Although a sandwich may be regarded as a very ordinary snack, it can be transformed into a luxurious and highly enjoyable meal, particularly with the addition of avocado, which could be easily classified as the food of the gods. Here are a few ideas for sandwich toppings and fillings, but the list goes on forever with each person's addition from their imaginative repertoire!

☐ Chicken, avocado and grain mustard
☐ Avocado, tomato, onion, cucumber, lettuce, grated carrot and mayonnaise
☐ Ham, avocado and tomato
☐ Avocado, alfalfa sprouts, cottage cheese and celery
☐ Banana and avocado, drizzled with honey
☐ Avocado, salmon, lettuce and mayonnaise
☐ Beetroot, avocado and cheese
☐ Hard-boiled egg, avocado and gherkin
☐ Avocado, cream cheese and olives
☐ Avocado, lemon juice, lettuce and tomato
☐ Cottage cheese, walnuts, avocado and celery

Grilled avocado and cheese on toast is another experience. Here are a number of combinations to have on toast:

☐ Chicken, avocado, lemon juice and cheese
☐ Ham, pineapple, avocado and cheese
☐ Avocado, tomato, ham and cheese
☐ Chicken, avocado, grain mustard and cheese
☐ Avocado, anchovy fillets and cheese
☐ Chutney, avocado and cheese

Avocado thinly sliced or mashed directly onto bread or toast is best when combined with the above ingredients.

When grilling avocado with cheese, vary your cheeses. For example, Edam or Gouda cheeses do not disintegrate as much as cheddar cheese, and they blend better with the subtleness of avocado. Mozzarella, Camembert or any of the herb cheeses are suitable too.

Vary the types of bread you use with avocado. There is nothing more delicious than avocado with thin slices of pumpernickel bread or rye bread. And, of course, all the fillings and toppings go equally as well with your favourite crispbread biscuits.

Sandwich Toppings and Fillings

AVOCADO STUFFED ROLLS

These rolls make a great lunch or snack.

4 large round wholewheat bread rolls
4 hard-boiled eggs, chopped
2 avocados, chopped
¾ cup grated cheese
2 tablespoons chopped capsicum
2 tablespoons finely chopped parsley
2 tablespoons tomato paste
2 tablespoons salad oil

Cut bread rolls in half. Scoop out insides, leaving a good crust. Mix all ingredients and stuff mix into roll cavity. Replace tops and wrap in foil.

Bake in moderate oven 180°C (350°F) for about 30 minutes.   Serves 4

Avocado Stuffed Rolls

STUFFED FRENCH BREADSTICK

Everyone loves garlic bread made with French loaves, but this recipe is just a bit different and will complement any meal. Make sure the avocado is not too ripe or it will brown.

1 avocado, mashed
little lemon juice
2 cloves garlic, crushed
2 tablespoons fresh chives, chopped
1 level teaspoon strong mustard
2 tablespoons grated fresh Parmesan cheese
    or 1 tablespoon packaged Parmesan
1 French breadstick

Mix all ingredients well and spread inside French breadstick sliced almost through.

Wrap in foil and heat in hot oven for 15 minutes, opening foil for last few minutes to allow bread to crisp slightly.

Herbed Avocado Cheese Damper

HERBED AVOCADO CHEESE DAMPER

4 cups self-raising flour (if
  using wholemeal flour,
  add 1 teaspoon baking
  powder)
1 teaspoon salt (optional)
1 large avocado, mashed
1 cup milk

½ cup water
½ cup fresh herbs (e.g.
  parsley, thyme,
  marjoram, basil, chives)
1 cup grated tasty cheese
½ teaspoon sweet paprika

Sift flour and baking powder, if used, into a large bowl.
Add 1 teaspoon salt if desired. Add mashed avocado and,
using fingertips, rub avocado in until mixture resembles
breadcrumbs.

Make a well in centre of mixture. Pour in milk and
water and chopped fresh herbs. Mix in quickly until it
forms a soft dough. Knead for a few minutes on a floured
board.

Gently form dough into a round or any desired shape
and place onto a greased and floured baking tray. Brush
top of damper with a little milk, sprinkle with cheese and
paprika, gently pushing cheese on top to stop from falling
off. Slit the top using a floured sharp knife.

Bake at 200°C (400°F) for approximately 25 minutes
and lower heat to 180°C (350°F) for a further 10 minutes.
Damper is cooked when it sounds hollow if gently
tapped.

Variation: 1 egg can be beaten and added when adding
milk, water and herbs.   Makes 1 damper

WHOLEMEAL AVOCADO SULTANA MUFFINS

There's nothing like muffins straight from the oven!

1½ cups wholemeal plain flour
2 level teaspoons baking powder
¼ teaspoon mixed spice
½ cup raw sugar
½ cup sultanas
1 large egg
¼ teaspoon vanilla essence
1 cup buttermilk
80 g soft butter
1 cup avocado, mashed

Sift flour with baking powder and mixed spice. Add sugar
and sultanas. Make a well in the centre.

Beat together egg, vanilla, buttermilk and soft butter
and mashed avocado. Pour into centre of dry ingredients
and mix enough just to blend in.

Spoon into greased muffin tins and bake at 190°C
(375°F) for 20–25 minutes until golden brown. Serve hot
with butter and honey.

Makes 1 dozen

AVOCADO 'BABY' SAVOURY

Once a baby is ready for solids, avocados provide an excellent source of protein, vitamins and minerals.

1 small carrot, grated
1 tablespoon alfalfa sprouts
1 very small lettuce leaf
juice 1 small orange
¼ medium-sized avocado
1 teaspoon tahini paste or peanut paste
sprig parsley

Blend carrot, sprouts, lettuce, orange juice until well pureed, stirring down occasionally.

Add avocado and tahini or peanut paste and parsley. Puree again until smooth.

Serves 1

AVOCADO 'BABY' SWEET

Any baby will love this treat. It's good for older children too.

¼ medium-sized avocado
2 dates, soaked overnight in water
½ banana
1 teaspoon finely ground sunflower seeds

Blend all ingredients in a blender or food processor until well combined. Add a little orange juice or water if too thick.

Serves 1

ALMOND AVOCADO MILK

about 600 mL milk
4 teaspoons ground raw almonds
2 teaspoons honey
1 teaspoon vanilla essence
1 avocado, chopped
nutmeg to garnish

Blend the milk, ground almonds, honey and vanilla for a couple of minutes in a blender.

With blender still in motion, drop chopped avocado through hole in lid and blend until smooth. The whip should be thick, but of pouring consistency (adjust with more milk).

Sprinkle with nutmeg to serve.

Serves 4

TROPICAL SUPERWHIP

1 avocado, chopped
1 banana, chopped
¼ cup pawpaw, chopped
2 teaspoons honey
2 teaspoons desiccated coconut
6 fresh mint leaves
600 mL orange juice or milk

Blend all ingredients and serve in very tall glasses, with a slice of kiwi fruit on the side of the glass. Decorate with a cocktail umbrella or fancy straw.

Serves 4

BANANNIE AVOCADO WHIP

1 large avocado, chopped
1 banana, chopped
2 teaspoons honey
1 teaspoon vanilla essence
3 glasses milk

Blend all ingredients in a blender until smooth and thick. Sprinkle with a little nutmeg to serve.   Serves 4

ORANGE AVOCADO AND YOGHURT WHIP

1 avocado, chopped coarsely
juice 2 oranges
1 dessertspoon honey
pinch cinnamon
2 dessertspoons natural yoghurt

Blend all ingredients and serve with crushed ice and an orange twist on the side of the glass.   Serves 2

EMERALD MILK WHIP

½ avocado, chopped
1 teaspoon honey
300 mL milk
2 scoops natural vanilla ice-cream
cinnamon to garnish

Blend all ingredients in blender and serve sprinkled with cinnamon.   Serves 2

(Left to right) Banannie Avocado Whip, Tropical Superwhip and Orange Avocado and Yoghurt Whip

DESSERTS

It may be difficult to imagine natural green desserts, but — apart from the spectacular colour of the avocado, which can be used to great effect to decorate, garnish or blend with other ingredients — the texture lends itself superbly to sweet dishes.
Included in this section are ice-creams, sorbets, cheesecakes, souffles, pancakes and gateaux. Banana is an excellent fruit to combine with avocado, both in texture and flavour. This combination has been used in the Banavo Pancake and suggested for the Avocado Ice Cream.
The subtle flavour of the avocado seems to be retained quite well in cooked desserts, such as the Passionfruit Avocado and Yoghurt Flan and the Custard and Avocado Tart. As previously mentioned, the uncooked avocado loses its colour and browns very easily and this should be borne in mind when preparing desserts such as the Date Avocado Tango and the Green Gateau.

CUSTARD AND AVOCADO TART

A tart with a rich pastry that can be served slightly warm or chilled.

PASTRY

60 g butter
125 g plain flour
2 egg yolks
1 whole egg
30 g raw sugar

FILLING

1 cup milk
1 cup cream
125 g raw sugar or honey
2 teaspoons vanilla essence
4 eggs, separated
1 large avocado (or 2 medium-sized)

Cut butter into flour and mix with fingertips until it develops a sandy texture. Mix egg yolks and egg with sugar and combine with flour mix. Form into a ball and refrigerate 30 minutes before using.

Grease a 20 cm pie dish and press pastry evenly in with fingertips over the bottom and sides. (This pastry has a very crumbly consistency and cannot be rolled.)

Prick all over with a fork and bake at 200°C (400°F) for only 5 minutes.

Blend all of the filling ingredients (except for the egg whites) in a blender until smooth.

Beat egg whites separately until soft peaks form; fold gently into custard with a metal spoon.

Pour filling into pastry case and bake at 180°C (350°F) for 20 to 30 minutes or until set.

Serve at room temperature with whipped cream or serve chilled.

Note: The cream can be sprinkled with a little ground cinnamon or nutmeg after garnishing the tart; alternatively, decorate by dusting icing sugar over a doily placed on the tart.

Serves 6–8

Custard and Avocado Tart

AVOCADO BAVAROIS ON A CRUST

The Bavarois, a creamy custard of eggs, milk and sugar, was created by a French chef in Bavaria. The smooth textures of the avocado and the custard are in delicious contrast to the crusty base.

CRUST

200 g shortbread biscuits
25 g desiccated coconut
1 teaspoon ground cinnamon
100 g unsalted butter, melted

Process the biscuits in a food processor until finely ground. Add the coconut, cinnamon and butter and mix well. Line a 22–24 cm round cheesecake tin with plastic wrap, extending over the side. Press the crumb mixture into the base of the tin, smooth the surface and then refrigerate while you make the Bavarois.

BAVAROIS

250 mL milk
1½ tablespoons gelatine
3 tablespoons hot water
4 egg yolks
1 cup caster sugar
1½ teaspoons vanilla essence
1 cup cream
approximately 380 g peeled avocado
juice of 1 large lime or small lemon

Put the milk in a heavy-based saucepan and bring to the boil over medium heat. Put the gelatine and hot water in a small bowl over a pan of simmering water and stir until dissolved.

Beat the egg yolks and sugar until light and creamy. Beat in the vanilla essence. Whisk in the hot milk gradually and then return the mixture to the heavy-based pan. Stir over low heat until the custard thickens so it will coat the back of a wooden spoon. Whisk in the dissolved gelatine. Cool quickly until lukewarm, either by putting in the refrigerator or over ice. Stir often.

Whip together the cream, avocado and lime or lemon juice in a food processor until completely smooth. Beat into the custard mixture and pour over the crumb base. Leave to set in the refrigerator for at least 4 hours or overnight.

Delicious served with fresh strawberries or kiwi fruit and whipped cream.

Note: The avocado should be slightly under-ripe but not hard. Eat the Bavarois within 2 days.

Serves 6–8

Passionfruit Avocado and Yoghurt Flan

PASSIONFRUIT AVOCADO AND YOGHURT FLAN

A highly nutritious dish that keeps well.

PASTRY	FILLING
200 g plain flour	*3 eggs*
50 g desiccated coconut	*5 tablespoons honey*
1 tablespoon sugar	*1 teaspoon vanilla*
125 g soft butter	*1½ cups natural yoghurt*
apple juice or water to	*2 large avocados, mashed*
moisten	*4 large passionfruit*

Mix flour, coconut and sugar. Cut in butter with long-bladed knife and rub with fingertips until it resembles breadcrumbs. Add enough apple juice or water to make dough come together.

Form a ball, wrap in plastic and refrigerate for at least 1 hour before using.

To make the filling, beat eggs, honey, vanilla and yoghurt. Mix mashed avocados and passionfruit pulp into egg mix.

Pour into prepared pastry case and bake at 180°C (350°F) for about 30 minutes until just set.

Cool and serve with whipped cream, extra passionfruit sprinkled with cinnamon, or nutmeg.

Serves 8–10

ZABAGLIONE CREAM SQUARES WITH AVOCADO

250 g puff pastry
2 avocados, very thinly
    sliced

ZABAGLIONE CREAM

3 egg yolks
2 tablespoons raw sugar
3 tablespoons Marsala wine
1 cup stiffly whipped cream

1 *Whisk until mixture becomes frothy, thick and rises*

Roll pastry out to a 23 cm square. Cut into 9 squares. Bake on a greased tray at 200°C (400°F) for 10 minutes or until lightly browned. Cool on a wire rack.

To make Zabaglione Cream, whisk all ingredients in a double boiler or heatproof bowl over simmering water. Continue whisking until mixture becomes frothy and thick and rises. Cool.

Fold through whipped cream. Refrigerate for 1 hour before using.

To serve, carefully cut each square of pastry in half. Pipe or spread the Zabaglione cream onto the bottom square and decorate with thinly sliced avocado. Replace pastry top. Finely chopped roasted almonds or hazelnuts can be sprinkled over the avocado before replacing the lid.

Note: Fruit juice can be substituted for the Marsala wine.

Serves 9

2 *Cut squares into halves, pipe cream onto bottom half*

Zabaglione Cream Squares with Avocado

CREAMED AVOCADO PUFFS

Everyone loves cream puffs, and with avocado filling they simply melt in the mouth.

PUFF MIXTURE

1 cup water
70 g butter, cut in small pieces
1 tablespoon raw sugar
1 cup sifted plain flour
4 eggs

FILLING

⅔ cup raw sugar
5 egg yolks
⅔ cup plain flour
1½ cups milk
1 teaspoon vanilla essence
2 cups chopped avocado
a little Creme de Menthe may be added
1 cup whipped cream sweetened with a little honey

GARNISH

avocado slices and finely sliced strawberries
icing sugar to dust

Place water, butter and sugar in pan and stir to completely melt butter. Bring to boil and remove from heat. Add flour all at once and stir vigorously. Reheat mixture for 2 minutes until the dough forms a ball.

Remove from heat and beat each egg well into mixture, one at a time. Butter and flour oven trays and, using 2 spoons, form balls about the size of an egg. Place 8 cm apart on tray.

Bake at 200°C (400°F) for 20 minutes or until puffed and golden brown.

To make the filling, beat sugar and yolks until thick and lemon coloured. Beat in flour. Heat milk and add to egg, sugar and flour mixture. Cook over moderate heat, stirring, to form a thick custard. Add vanilla and cool.

Mash avocados with Creme de Menthe and cream.

Slice top of each puff. Fill with cooled custard and remaining space with avocado cream. Garnish with avocado slices and finely sliced strawberries. Replace cream puff lid. Dust with sifted icing sugar before serving.

Serves 8

Creamed Avocado Puffs

GREEN-WITH-ENVY CHEESECAKE

Cheesecake is loved by all, and with this avocado filling it will be even more popular.

2 cups fine biscuit crumbs
½ cup melted butter
3 tablespoons raw sugar
500 g cream cheese
3 avocados
1 cup cream
3 eggs
1 cup honey or raw sugar
½ teaspoon cinnamon
1 teaspoon vanilla essence
¼ cup brandy
whipped cream and kiwifruit slices to garnish

Mix biscuit crumbs with the melted butter and sugar, working it together with your fingers. Press into well-greased spring-form tin and, using a masher, make a flat, smooth crust.

Beat cream cheese with avocados, cream, eggs, honey or sugar until smooth. This can be done in a blender, electric mixer or food processor. Add cinnamon, vanilla and brandy.

Pour mixture into prepared spring-form pan and bake at 160°C (310°F) for about 1 hour.

Cool, refrigerate and garnish with whipped cream and kiwifruit before serving.

Serves 12

Green-with-Envy Cheesecake

SOUR CREAM AVODAMIA PIE

CRUST	FILLING
80 g roasted macadamia nuts, ground (other nuts can be substituted)	300 mL sour cream
	200 g sugar
	2 tablespoons cornflour
130 g plain flour	4 egg yolks
60 g caster sugar	1 teaspoon vanilla essence
125 g butter	2 avocados, mashed
water	2 teaspoons gelatine
20 g roasted macadamia nuts for garnish	3 tablespoons hot water

Mix ground nuts with flour and sugar. Cut small pieces of softened butter into dry ingredients and rub in with fingertips until it resembles breadcrumbs. Mix in enough water to make soft dough.

Press into sides and base of a 20 cm pie dish. Bake at 180°C (350°F) for approximately 25 minutes. Cool.

To make the filling, heat sour cream in a double boiler until warm. Stir in sugar and cornflour. Then stir in lightly beaten egg yolks. Blend well, then bring to boil. Simmer 20 minutes.

Remove from heat and add vanilla essence and mashed avocado. Dissolve gelatine with hot water and add to mixture. Mix well.

Spoon into crust and chill. Before serving, garnish top with chopped, roasted macadamia nuts.

Serves 8

Sour Cream Avodamia Pie

HAZELNUT AVOCADO CHARLOTTE

Here is a variation of a wonderful French dessert, which can look as if it was prepared by a top French chef if you allow a little time and patience.

14 ladyfinger biscuits
¾ cup whipped cream
chopped hazelnuts for
    garnish
½ avocado, for garnish

VANILLA SAUCE	HAZELNUT AVOCADO CREAM
2 cups milk	
1 vanilla bean, split	1½ teaspoons gelatine
6 egg yolks	2 tablespoons water
⅔ cup sugar	300 mL cream
1½ tablespoons gelatine, softened in 2 tablespoons water	2 avocados
	1 teaspoon vanilla essence
	⅓ cup sugar
	⅔ cup ground hazelnuts (raw or roasted)

First make the Vanilla Sauce.

Put milk and vanilla bean in a saucepan and heat gently. When it comes to the boil, remove from heat, cover and leave for 10 minutes for vanilla bean to infuse.

Beat egg yolks and sugar until the mixture forms a trail. Continue beating and add milk, after removing vanilla bean. Pour mixture back into saucepan, heat slowly while stirring with a wooden spoon and do not allow to boil.

When sauce coats the back of spoon, remove from heat and place pan in a bowl of cold water to stop it cooking further. Remove vanilla bean. Stir sauce occasionally as it cools. While still warm, add softened gelatine.

To prepare the Hazelnut Avocado Cream, soften gelatine in 2 tablespoons water and dissolve over a saucepan of hot water. Cool, but do not allow to set.

Blend cream, avocados, vanilla and sugar in a blender until smooth and thick, blending in softened gelatine at the end. Pour into a bowl and fold through ground hazelnuts.

To assemble the dessert, grease a 16 cm charlotte mould with butter and line the sides with ladyfinger biscuits, cutting them off at the rim if they stick up. Fill mould half full with Hazelnut Avocado Cream and refrigerate for 30 minutes. Then pour Vanilla Sauce over Hazelnut Avocado Cream and refrigerate for at least 1 hour.

To turn out, dip mould into hot water for only a few seconds and turn it upside down on a platter. Decorate with whipped cream, coarsely chopped hazelnuts, and a star shape made of avocado slices on top.

Serves 6–8

AVOCADO TOFFEE SHORTCAKE

The special addition of toffee sweetens the avocado in this shortcake — always a favourite to serve with coffee or tea.

2 cups sifted plain flour
4 teaspoons baking powder
2 tablespoons caster sugar
⅓ cup unsalted butter
1 egg
½ cup milk
1 cup cream, whipped stiffly with 1 teaspoon
   vanilla essence
2 avocados, sliced thinly or diced

Sift flour with baking powder and sugar. Cut in butter until mixture resembles breadcrumbs.

Beat egg with milk and add quickly to dry ingredients, taking care not to overmix. Roll out to a thickness of about 1 cm on a floured board and cut into rounds with a floured 6 cm scone cutter or a glass.

Put rounds on a greased baking tray and bake at 220°C (425°F) for 10–15 minutes or until golden and slightly puffed. Cool slightly and split in half. On each shortcake bottom spread some whipped cream, cover with avocado and sprinkle over coarsely crushed toffee. Replace shortcake lid, decorate with another spoonful of cream, an avocado slice and some more toffee.

TOFFEE

1¼ cups granulated sugar
⅓ cup water
½ teaspoon lemon juice

Place sugar and water in a heavy-bottomed saucepan and place over moderate heat. Heat, stirring with a wooden spoon and, just before it boils, add lemon juice.

When syrup boils, stop stirring it. Continue boiling and test it with a candy thermometer until temperature reaches 156°C (314°F). Toffee burns beyond this temperature.

Make sure thermometer does not touch bottom or sides of pan in which you are cooking syrup. Once syrup reaches desired temperature, pour onto oiled baking sheet. When cold, break toffee up into small bits and crush.

1 *Pour toffee into tray to set*

2 *Spread with cream, avocado and toffee*

Avocado Toffee Shortcake

GREEN GATEAU

Be adventurous! Try this delicious sponge, layered and iced in delicate green!

SPONGE

6 egg yolks
1 cup fine raw sugar (finely ground in a blender)
3 tablespoons cold water
grated rind 1 lemon
1 tablespoon lemon juice
1 teaspoon vanilla essence
8 egg whites, beaten, stiff but not dry
1½ cups plain wholemeal flour

FILLING

½ large avocado
150 mL stiffly whipped cream
honey to sweeten

TOPPING

1 avocado
150 mL stiffly whipped cream
honey to sweeten
½ teaspoon vanilla essence

GARNISH

4 tablespoons unsalted pepitas
½ cup unsalted pistachio nuts, finely ground
½ avocado, thinly sliced

Beat yolks until light and creamy. Add sugar, 2 tablespoons at a time, beating constantly. Beat until sugar is well combined. Add water, 1 tablespoon at a time. Then add rind and juice with vanilla.

Beat whites and place on top of mixture. Sift flour on top. Carefully fold it all together with a large metal spoon until combined. Spoon into greased 25 cm cake tin or spring-form tin and bake at 170°C (325°F) for about 1 hour (or until a skewer inserted in centre comes out clean).

Run a knife around edge and gently empty onto cake rack to cool. Cut in half.

To make the filling, mash avocado and mix well into whipped cream with honey. Spread over top of the bottom half of the cut cake. Put top on.

For the topping, mash avocado and mix well into whipped cream with honey and vanilla. Spread over top of cake and around sides.

To garnish, gently press pepitas onto top or sides of cake. Decorate top of cake around the edges with ground pistachio nuts and in the centre, with the sliced avocado.

Whipped cream can be piped around edge of cake and nuts sprinkled on centre part. Optional: chocolate shavings can be sprinkled over the cake if desired.

Note: With this recipe you can substitute your favourite sponge cake and use the given filling and topping.

Serves 8–10

Green Gateau

FRENCH AVOCADO GATEAU

A choux pastry served in a spectacular symphony of greens.

PASTRY

120 g butter
2 cups water
2 tablespoons raw sugar
2 cups plain flour
8 eggs

FILLING

3 avocados, beaten with 4 tablespoons honey until
*   smooth and creamy*
2 cups stiffly whipped cream
2 small bunches green grapes, seedless

Chop butter into small pieces and melt it with the water and sugar. Bring to the boil and remove from heat. Add flour all at once and stir vigorously.

Return to heat and cook further over moderate heat until pastry forms a ball.

Remove from heat and stir in eggs, one at a time, beating well.

Grease and flour 3 round pie dishes. Divide mixture equally between the dishes and spread evenly over, leaving about 2 cm between edge of pie dish and pastry. Bake at 180°C (350°F) for 20 minutes. Turn oven off and leave in further 5 minutes. Remove from oven and cool.

For the filling, mix avocado and honey with whipped cream until well blended. Pull grapes from stems and wash well.

To serve, spread each choux ring with avocado cream and decorate with grapes. Put the layers of choux pastry onto each other to form a gateau. Pipe a little avocado cream around the edge of the top ring. Cut into cake wedges.

Serves 8

GREEN VELVET MERINGUE ROLL

Soft meringue filled with a smooth avocado centre and topped with cream and passionfruit.

MERINGUE ROLL

5 egg whites
1 cup caster sugar
1 teaspoon vanilla essence
1 teaspoon vinegar

FILLING

1 cup cream
1 ½ large avocados, chopped
1 tablespoon honey

GARNISH

½ cup whipped cream
½ avocado, mashed
3 large passionfruit

Line a greased Swiss roll tin with greased greaseproof paper. Beat egg whites until stiff and peaks form. Gradually beat in sugar until dissolved. Beat in vanilla and vinegar. Spread mixture evenly into prepared tin and bake at 200°C (400°F) for 10 minutes, or until firm to touch and a pale golden colour. Turn out onto greaseproof paper sprinkled with sifted icing sugar and stand for 2 minutes.

To make the filling, blend cream, avocados and honey in blender or food processor until a smooth, creamy consistency is achieved. Spread over slightly cooled meringue and roll up lengthways with the aid of the greaseproof paper. Put onto serving platter with sealed side underneath.

Whip cream and mashed avocado together. Pipe whipped avocado cream on top of meringue roll and top with passionfruit pulp.

Serves 8–10

ALMONDINE AVOCADO MERINGUE

4 egg whites
1 cup caster sugar
1 cup roasted almonds, finely chopped or ground
1¼ cups cream
1 teaspoon vanilla essence
2 avocados, mashed, with 2 tablespoons honey
50 g dark chocolate, melted in double boiler

Line two baking trays with non-stick baking paper. Draw an 18 cm ring on each.

Whisk egg whites until very stiff and holding peaks. Whisk in 1 tablespoon of sugar, then fold in remaining sugar with a metal spoon.

Sprinkle over ¾ cup of roasted almonds and very quickly cut them into the meringue.

Spoon half of the mixture on to the prepared tray, mounding up the sides a little, and the other half onto the other tray.

The meringue, which will go on top to assemble, should be peaked a little.

Bake at 160°C (310°F) for 35 to 40 minutes or until firm and lightly golden.

Peel off baking paper and replace, upside down, into oven to cool with door open slightly.

To assemble, sandwich the meringue together with a layer of cream whipped with vanilla, and a layer of avocado puree. Decorate the top of the meringue with melted chocolate and refrigerate about 30 minutes before serving.
Serves 6–8

SWEET CREPE BATTER

Dessert crepes and pancakes are always popular, and avocados make them special. This batter recipe is basic for all dessert crepes, and will make about 16 crepes.

1¼ cups milk
1 egg, whole
1 egg yolk
20 g butter, melted
2 tablespoons raw sugar
1 cup plain flour

Blend all ingredients in a blender. Turn off and stir down flour. Blend again and then stand in refrigerator 1 hour before using.

Use a small amount of butter to grease a heavy frypan or crepe pan and allow pan to get fairly hot before pouring in batter.

For a crepe, don't pour too much mixture in. Tilt the pan as you do it to shape the crepe into a round. It is ready to turn when little bubbles appear on the surface.

Note: Unfilled crepes or pancakes can be frozen. Allow to cool, one by one, before placing them in freezer. Once frozen, they thaw out very quickly.

Makes 16

Almondine Avocado Meringue

BANAVO CREPE

2 avocados
2 bananas
2 tablespoons honey
juice ½ lemon
4 prepared crepes (see Sweet Crepe Batter)
½ teaspoon cinnamon
1 teaspoon raw sugar

Mash avocado and banana with honey and lemon juice. Spread over half of cooked crepe. Fold over and quickly brown in butter on both sides until heated through.

Sprinkle with cinnamon and sugar to serve, and cream or ice cream if desired. Slices of avocado or banana can provide an excellent finishing touch.

Serves 4

Grand Marnier Avocado Crepe

GRAND MARNIER AVOCADO CREPE

Sweet Crepe Batter (see recipe)
4 avocados, thinly sliced
whipped cream to serve
thin strips of glazed orange slices to garnish

SAUCE

60 g unsalted butter
juice 2 oranges
grated rind 1 orange
3 tablespoons raw sugar or honey
2 tablespoons Grand Marnier

Make crepes and roll into cylinders with thinly sliced avocado inside.

To make sauce, heat butter in frying pan and stir in juice, rind and sugar or honey. Cook a minute or two over a gentle heat.

Add crepe cylinders to sauce and cook gently on all sides.

Decorate with glazed orange slices.

Add Grand Marnier and flame. Serve, while alight, with cream in a separate dish.   Makes 16

TROPICAL CREME CARAMEL

A variation to a traditional dessert — an avocado touch served with tropical fruits. This recipe can be made a day ahead.

CARAMEL

¾ cup raw sugar
1 cup water

CUSTARD

4 eggs
2 egg yolks
1 teaspoon vanilla essence or vanilla bean
¼ cup raw sugar
1½ cups mashed avocado
2 cups milk

TOPPING

¼ avocado, finely sliced
½ mango, finely diced
½ kiwi fruit, finely sliced
½ large banana, finely sliced
1 teaspoon finely sliced pawpaw
300 mL cream, whipped

Stir sugar and water over low heat until sugar dissolves. Bring to boil, without stirring, and cook until a rich golden brown. Don't stir.

Pour caramel evenly into individual souffle dishes and, working very fast, revolve dishes in order to coat sides and base. Use an oven glove as dishes become quite hot when coating with caramel.

Place eggs, egg yolks, vanilla and sugar in a bowl and beat together lightly. Beat in mashed avocado until smooth and creamy.

Heat milk and bring to just below boiling point. (If using vanilla bean, heat bean with milk.) Cool 10 minutes and add vanilla essence.

Pour milk over egg and avocado mixture, stirring constantly. Strain if any large lumps occur.

Place caramel-lined dishes in a baking tray. Add water to tray so that it is half-way up sides of dishes. Pour in custard and bake in 160°C (310°F) oven for about 30 to 35 minutes or until custard is set.

Cover each dish with foil and refrigerate several hours before serving.

Combine topping fruits.

To serve, ease custard away from sides of dish with fingers. Turn out onto individual small plates or saucers. Decorate with whipped cream piped around edge of custard. Fill centre with colourful array of chopped fruits.

Alternatively top with whipped cream and serve fruits alongside.

Serves 6

1 *Revolve dishes to coat sides and base with caramel*

2 *Pour milk over egg and avocado mixture*

3 *Pour custard into dishes prior to baking*

Tropical Creme Caramel

CHOCOLATE AVOCADO SWIRL

1 large avocado
1 teaspoon vanilla essence
2 teaspoons honey
1 cup whipped cream
40 g dark chocolate, melted
30 g dark chocolate curls

Mash avocado with vanilla and honey. Fold through whipped cream. Slowly pour cooled, melted chocolate into avocado cream. Stir in slightly so as to give a streaky look.

Put into tall parfait glasses or bowls and garnish with curls.

Note: To accentuate the chocolate swirl, use a piping bag with a very fine attachment and make a spiral design on the inside of the glass. Allow to set and gently spoon in avocado mixture.

Serves 2

Chocolate Avocado Swirl

Date Avocado Tango

DATE AVOCADO TANGO

This dish is similar to a mousse, but with more 'goodies'.

2 avocados, mashed
2 tablespoons honey
juice and rind 1 orange
4 tablespoons chopped dates
150 mL whipped cream
2 egg whites, stiffly beaten

Mix well avocado, honey, orange juice, rind and dates. Fold whipped cream through (stiffly) and then egg whites (gently) with a metal spoon.

Serve in individual bowls and garnish with very thin strips of orange rind (cooked in honey and water-syrup until soft).

Decorate with more whipped cream around the edges if desired.

Serves 4

AVOCADO MAPLE WAFFLES

WAFFLES

2 cups self-raising flour
½ teaspoon salt
2 eggs, beaten
1½ cups milk
3 tablespoons melted butter

FILLING

1 cup mashed avocado
⅓ cup caster sugar
¾ cup cream
pure maple syrup, to taste
1 cup walnut pieces
icing sugar, to garnish

Heat the waffle maker. Place the flour and salt in a large bowl and make a well in the centre. Mix together the eggs, milk and butter and pour into the dry ingredients; whisk until smooth. Pour ½ cup of batter into the lightly greased waffle maker and cook for 1–2 minutes. Repeat with the remaining batter (this should make 4–6 waffles).

Put the avocado, caster sugar and cream in a blender or food processor and mix until smooth and thick. Put into a piping bag and pipe in mounds over the waffles. Drizzle with maple syrup and scatter with walnut pieces. Dust with icing sugar to serve.

Serves 4–6

LIMORANGE AVOCADO SORBET

A sorbet with the consistency of gelato and a tangy flavour that makes it ideal in hot weather.

1½ cups avocado puree
¼ cup cream
4 tablespoons honey
1¼ cups fresh orange juice
juice 1 lime or lemon
2 egg whites, stiffly beaten

Blend (in a blender) the avocado, cream and honey until smooth. Mix orange and lime or lemon juices together and fold through avocado puree. Gently fold through egg whites with a metal spoon.

Freeze and when almost frozen, mix and refreeze.

Note: Remove sorbet from freezer a little before needed so it can soften slightly.

Serves about 6

LEMON AVOCADO SOUFFLE

A rich, beautiful and tasty end to a meal.

4 egg yolks
200 g raw sugar
2 lemons
2 tablespoons gelatine or agar-agar
300 mL cream
3 avocados
6 egg whites
avocado slices and a lemon twist to garnish

Beat egg yolks and sugar together. Grate rinds of lemons and squeeze the juice. Add rind and 6 tablespoons of lemon juice to egg yolks, beating constantly.

Soften gelatine in 6 tablespoons water and heat until it is liquid. Do the same if using agar-agar. Cool slightly.

Whip cream and beat into mashed avocados. Then stir into lemon and egg mixture.

Stir in gelatine and continue until it begins to thicken.

Beat egg whites until soft peaks form. Fold into lemon and avocado mixture.

Spoon carefully into a souffle dish or tall parfait glasses and chill until set.

Note: This souffle can be served with extra whipped cream and garnished with avocado slices, a lemon twist and a sprig of mint.

Serves 10

LEMON AVOCADO GELATO

The taste and texture of this is very similar to gelato and has a delicious lemony tang and vivid green colour. Try scooping it into ice cream cones.

250 g whole avocados
½ cup lemon juice
150 g caster sugar
250 g natural yoghurt

Put the avocado, lemon juice, sugar and yoghurt in a food processor or blender and mix until smooth. Freeze in a small ice cream container or freezer bowl. Stir once or twice during freezing.

Makes 500 mL

AVOCADO ICE CREAM

Ice cream goes with so many things and is much nicer and more nutritious if you make it yourself. The subtle taste and the green colour of the avocado makes this a truly unique ice cream.

2 large avocados
3 cups cream
6 tablespoons honey
2 teaspoons vanilla essence
3 bananas (if unavailable, add one extra avocado)
3 egg whites, stiffly beaten

Blend avocado, cream, honey, vanilla and banana in small batches in blender until thick. Pour into ice cream tray or container.

Beat egg whites and fold into ice cream carefully with a metal spoon. Freeze.

Gently stir ice cream when it is starting to freeze around the edges. Repeat twice more and then allow ice cream to freeze.

Remove from freezer about 20 minutes before serving. Serve with fresh sliced strawberries and kiwifruit.

Note: This recipe makes about 2 litres. It can be made in a commercial ice cream maker, but I find the above method easy and successful. The key to a good consistency is ensuring that the mixture is beaten initially until thick, and also that the ice cream is mixed as it freezes to prevent ice crystals forming.

AVOCADO ICE CREAM SPLIT

This dish is a great favourite with children.

1 avocado, sliced lengthways into 4 pieces
4 scoops Avocado Ice Cream
4–6 tablespoons pure maple syrup
2 tablespoons crushed nuts
fresh strawberries, kiwifruit or cherries

Place sliced avocado along sides of long shallow glass dish. Fill centre with ice cream scoops. Spoon over maple syrup and sprinkle with nuts. Garnish with strawberries, cherries or kiwifruit.

Serves 2

Avocado Ice Cream Split

SICILIAN AVOCADO CASSATA

All the delicacies of true Italian cassata ice cream made even more luscious with avocado.

FIRST LAYER

2 eggs, separated
1 cup cream
3 dessertspoons honey
1 teaspoon almond essence

SECOND LAYER

1 cup cream
2 large avocados
4 dessertspoons honey
1 teaspoon vanilla essence
60 g chopped toasted almonds
8 tablespoons mixed glazed fruit
2 egg whites

THIRD LAYER

2 eggs, separated
1 cup cream
3 dessertspoons honey
2 dessertspoons Marsala wine
80 g dark chocolate, melted in double boiler or
*   heatproof bowl over simmering water*

To make the first layer, beat egg whites until soft peaks form. Fold in lightly beaten egg yolks. Beat cream until very stiff. Beat in honey. Add almond essence and then fold mixture into beaten eggs. Pour into 20 cm round cake tin and spread top out evenly. Freeze.

For the second layer, beat together cream, avocado and honey in blender until smooth and thick. Add vanilla essence. Mix in toasted almonds and glazed fruit. Beat egg whites and fold gently into cream mixture. Spread evenly over frozen first layer and freeze again.

Make the third layer by beating egg whites until soft peaks form. Beat cream until very stiff, and whip in honey and Marsala. Mix slightly cooled melted chocolate into cream and combine well. Gently fold beaten egg yolks into chocolate cream and then beaten egg whites. Spread evenly over second layer and freeze again.

To serve, turn cake tin onto large round plate. Gently rub a hot cloth over surface and sides of tin. The ice cream should drop out on to the plate like a cake.

If you have difficulty, run a knife around the edge of the cake tin and then rub a hot cloth over the surface of the tin.

Note: This looks wonderful when served at a dinner party garnished with fresh flowers or maraschino stemmed cherries. It is also a nice change for Christmas dinner dessert if you tire of the traditional plum pudding. The cassata can be placed in the freezer on its serving platter ready for use.

Serves 10

MINTED AVOCADO CREAMS WITH KIWI SAUCE

This is a very quick dessert to prepare.

3 teaspoons gelatine	KIWI SAUCE
1 tablespoon water	
1½ cups cream	3 kiwifruit
⅓ cup honey	¼ cup light fruit juice
1 large avocado	(apple or pineapple)
2 teaspoons finely chopped	1 tablespoon honey
fresh mint	
1 tablespoon lemon or lime	
juice	
1 kiwifruit and mint leaves	
for decoration	

Sprinkle gelatine over water and dissolve over hot water. Cool slightly. Blend cream, honey, avocado, mint and lemon or lime juice until smooth in blender or food processor. Be careful not to over blend as mixture curdles easily. Add dissolved gelatine and mix well. Spoon mixture into 4 lightly oiled small moulds. Refrigerate until set (about 2 hours).

Blend all ingredients for the sauce in a blender until well combined for a sauce consistency.

To serve, pour some of Kiwi Sauce on 6 bread and butter plates or pretty saucers. Unmould avocado creams into centre of each plate and garnish with sliced kiwifruit and mint leaves, or other decorative leaves of your choice.

Note: Individual jelly moulds can be used for the cream moulds.

Serves 4

AVOCADO YOGHURT DESSERT LOAF

Weight-conscious people will love this healthful, yoghurt-based, ice cream loaf.

1 large avocado	2 teaspoons grated orange
400 g low-fat plain yoghurt	rind
2 tablespoons honey	1 egg white
½ teaspoon vanilla essence	

Mash avocado with a little of the yoghurt or blend in a blender until smooth. Combine the remaining yoghurt, honey, vanilla essence and orange rind with the avocado and mix well.

Pour into loaf tray and freeze for about 1 hour, or until mixture is beginning to set.

Beat ice cream to mix in the ice crystals. Beat egg white until stiff and fold gently into ice cream. Return to freezer after smoothing ice cream evenly on top. Freeze until set.

Serves 4

AVOCADO DREAM SALAD

1 large avocado, chopped	2 kiwifruit, chopped
2 bananas, chopped	2 mangos, chopped
1 small pawpaw	juice 1 orange
(approximately 2 cups	toasted coconut shreds, for
chopped)	garnish
3 passionfruit	

Toss all fruits together gently with orange juice. Spoon into bowls and top with Avocado Dream Cream if desired. Garnish with toasted coconut shreds.

AVOCADO DREAM CREAM

1 avocado
2 bananas
1 teaspoon honey
½ cup water or fruit juice

Blend all ingredients in a blender or food processor until smooth, adding a little extra water or fruit juice if too stiff. Allow cream to be fairly thick as it does not need to have a pouring consistency.

Serves 4

ISLAND MOUSSE

A sea of green with green islands. Individual avocado mousses with a sauce of coconut milk and Creme de Menthe.

2 egg yolks	SAUCE
¼ cup sugar	
2 teaspoons gelatine	150 mL coconut milk
1 tablespoon water	150 mL stiffly whipped
½ cup whipped cream	cream
1 large avocado	1½ tablespoons Creme de
3 egg whites	Menthe
pinch salt	

Put egg yolks and sugar in top of double boiler and beat over simmering water until mixture thickens. Dissolve gelatine in one tablespoon cold water over hot water. Cool.

Blend cream in blender with avocado until smooth. Add cooled gelatine to egg mixture and fold in cream and avocado.

Beat egg whites with a pinch of salt until soft peaks form. Fold gently into mixture. Spoon mixture into four lightly greased moulds (heart shaped look very nice) and refrigerate for several hours or overnight.

Put all sauce ingredients in blender or food processor and blend until thick.

To serve, unmould mousse onto dessert plate and pour sauce around mousse. Decorate with a tropical flower.

Serves 4

INDEX

MEASURING MADE EASY

HOW TO MEASURE DRY INGREDIENTS

15 g	½ oz	
30 g	1 oz	
60 g	2 oz	
90 g	3 oz	
125 g	4 oz	(¼ lb)
155 g	5 oz	
185 g	6 oz	
220 g	7 oz	
250 g	8 oz	(½ lb)
280 g	9 oz	
315 g	10 oz	
345 g	11 oz	
375 g	12 oz	(¾ lb)
410 g	13 oz	
440 g	14 oz	
470 g	15 oz	
500 g	16 oz	(1 lb)
750 g	24 oz	(1½ lb)
1 kg	32 oz	(2 lb)

QUICK CONVERSIONS

5 mm	¼ inch	
1 cm	½ inch	
2 cm	¾ inch	
2.5 cm	1 inch	
5 cm	2 inches	
6 cm	2½ inches	
8 cm	3 inches	
10 cm	4 inches	
12 cm	5 inches	
15 cm	6 inches	
18 cm	7 inches	
20 cm	8 inches	
23 cm	9 inches	
25 cm	10 inches	
28 cm	11 inches	
30 cm	12 inches	(1 foot)
46 cm	18 inches	
50 cm	20 inches	
61 cm	24 inches	(2 feet)
77 cm	30 inches	

NOTE: We developed the recipes in this book in Australia where the tablespoon measure is 20 ml. In many other countries the tablespoon is 15 ml. For most recipes this difference will not be noticeable.

However, for recipes using baking powder, gelatine, bicarbonate of soda, small amounts of flour and cornflour, we suggest you add an extra teaspoon for each tablespoon specified.

Many people find it very convenient to use cup measurements. You can buy special measuring cups or measure water in an ordinary household cup to check it holds 250 ml (8 fl oz). This can then be used for both liquid and dry cup measurements.

MEASURING LIQUIDS

METRIC CUPS

¼ cup	60 ml	2 fluid ounces
⅓ cup	80 ml	2½ fluid ounces
½ cup	125 ml	4 fluid ounces
¾ cup	180 ml	6 fluid ounces
1 cup	250 ml	8 fluid ounces

METRIC SPOONS

¼ teaspoon	1.25 ml
½ teaspoon	2.5 ml
1 teaspoon	5 ml
1 tablespoon	20 ml

OVEN TEMPERATURES

TEMPERATURES	CELSIUS (°C)	FAHRENHEIT (°F)	GAS MARK
Very Slow	120	250	½
Slow	150	300	2
Moderate	160-180	325-350	3-4
Moderately hot	190-200	375-400	5-6
Hot	220-230	425-450	7-8
Very hot	250-260	475-500	9-10

Published by Murdoch Books®,
a division of Murdoch Magazines Pty Ltd,
213 Miller Street, North Sydney NSW 2060.

Jacket Design: Sylvie Abecassis.
Cover and some internal photography by Chris Jones,
with styling by Mary Harris and food preparation by Alison Turner.
Front cover: Warm Tuna, Avocado and Potato Salad (page 33).
Back cover: Barramundi and Avocado Provencale (page 39).

Managing Editor: Jane Price.
Food Editors: Kerrie Ray, Tracy Rutherford.
CEO & Publisher: Anne Wilson.
International Sales Director: Mark Newman.

National Library of Australia Cataloguing-in-Publication Data:
Heaslip, Christine. The complete avocado cookbook. Rev. ed.
Includes index. ISBN 0 86411 558 X. 1. Cookery (Avocado).
I. Title. (Series: Bay Books cookery collection). 641.64653.
First published in Australia in 1984. Revised edition 1988, reprinted 1992,
1993. This edition first printed 1997.
Printed by Toppan Printing (S) Pte. Ltd, Singapore.